0

MATHEMATICS IN SPORT

ELLIS HORWOOD SERIES IN
MATHEMATICS AND ITS APPLICATIONS
Series Editor: Professor G. M. BELL, Chelsea College, University of London

Statistics and Operational Research
Editor: B. W. CONOLLY, Chelsea College, University of London

Baldock, G. R. & Bridgeman, T.	Mathematical Theory of Wave Motion
de Barra, G.	Measure Theory and Integration
Berry, J. S., Burghes, D. N., Huntley, I. D., James, D. J. G. & Moscardini, A. O.	
	Teaching and Applying Mathematical Modelling
Burghes, D. N. & Borrie, M.	Modelling with Differential Equations
Burghes, D. N. & Downs, A. M.	Modern Introduction to Classical Mechanics and Control
Burghes, D. N. & Graham, A.	Introduction to Control Theory, including Optimal Control
Burghes, D. N., Huntley, I. & McDonald, J.	Applying Mathematics
Burghes, D. N. & Wood, A. D.	Mathematical Models in the Social, Management and Life Sciences
Butkovskiy, A. G.	Green's Functions and Transfer Functions Handbook
Butkovskiy, A. G.	Structure of Distributed Systems
Chorlton, F.	Textbook of Dynamics, 2nd Edition
Chorlton, F.	Vector and Tensor Methods
Dunning-Davies, J.	Mathematical Methods for Mathematicians, Physical Scientists and Engineers
Eason, G., Coles, C. W. & Gettinby, G.	Mathematics and Statistics for the Bio-sciences
Exton, H.	Handbook of Hypergeometric Integrals
Exton, H.	Multiple Hypergeometric Functions and Applications
Exton, H.	*q*-Hypergeometric Functions and Applications
Faux, I. D. & Pratt, M. J.	Computational Geometry for Design and Manufacture
Firby, P. A. & Gardiner, C. F.	Surface Topology
Gardiner, C. F.	Modern Algebra
Gasson, P. C.	Geometry of Spatial Forms
Goodbody, A. M.	Cartesian Tensors
Goult, R. J.	Applied Linear Algebra
Graham, A.	Kronecker Products and Matrix Calculus: with Applications
Graham, A.	Matrix Theory and Applications for Engineers and Mathematicians
Griffel, D. H.	Applied Functional Analysis
Hoskins, R. F.	Generalised Functions
Hunter, S. C.	Mechanics of Continuous Media, 2nd (Revised) Edition
Huntley, I. & Johnson, R. M.	Linear and Nonlinear Differential Equations
Jaswon, M. A. & Rose, M. A.	Crystal Symmetry: The Theory of Colour Crystallography
Kim, K. H. & Roush, F. W.	Applied Abstract Algebra
Kosinski, W.	Field Singularities and Wave Analysis in Continuum Mechanics
Marichev, O. I.	Integral Transforms of Higher Transcendental Functions
Meek, B. L. & Fairthorne, S.	Using Computers
Muller-Pfeiffer, E.	Spectral Theory of Ordinary Differential Operators
Nonweiler, T. R. F.	Computational Mathematics: An Introduction to Numerical Analysis
Oldknow, A. & Smith, D.	Learning Mathematics with Micros
Ogden, R. W.	Non-linear Elastic Deformations
Ratschek, H. & Rokne, Jon	Computer Methods for the Range of Functions
Scorer, R. S.	Environmental Aerodynamics
Schendel, U.	Introduction to Parallel Processors
Smith, D. K.	Network Optimisation Practice: A Computational Guide
Srivastava, H. M. & Manocha, H. L.	A Treatise on Generating Functions
Sweet, M. V.	Algebra, Geometry and Trigonometry for Science Students
Temperley, H. N. V. & Trevena, D. H.	Liquids and Their Properties
Temperley, H. N. V.	Graph Theory and Applications
Thom, R.	Mathematical Models of Morphogenesis
Thomas, L. C.	Games Theory and Applications
Townend, M. Stewart	Mathematics in Sport
Twizell, E. H.	Computational Methods for Partial Differential Equations
Wheeler, R. F.	Rethinking Mathematical Concepts
Willmore, T. J.	Total Curvature in Riemannian Geometry
Willmore, T. J. & Hitchin, N.	Global Riemannian Geometry

MATHEMATICS IN SPORT

M. STEWART TOWNEND, B.Sc., M.Sc.
Senior Lecturer, Department of Mathematics
Liverpool Polytechnic

ELLIS HORWOOD LIMITED
Publishers · Chichester

Halsted Press: a division of
JOHN WILEY & SONS
New York · Chichester · Brisbane · Toronto

First published in 1984 by
ELLIS HORWOOD LIMITED
Market Cross House, Cooper Street, Chichester, West Sussex, PO19 1EB, England

The publisher's colophon is reproduced from James Gillison's drawing of the ancient Market Cross, Chichester.

Distributors:

Australia, New Zealand, South-east Asia:
Jacaranda-Wiley Ltd., Jacaranda Press,
JOHN WILEY & SONS INC.,
G.P.O. Box 859, Brisbane, Queensland 40001, Australia

Canada:
JOHN WILEY & SONS CANADA LIMITED
22 Worcester Road, Rexdale, Ontario, Canada.

Europe, Africa:
JOHN WILEY & SONS LIMITED
Baffins Lane, Chichester, West Sussex, England.

North and South America and the rest of the world:
Halsted Press: a division of
JOHN WILEY & SONS
605 Third Avenue, New York, N.Y. 10016, U.S.A.

© 1984 M.S. Townend/Ellis Horwood Limited

British Library Cataloguing in Publication Data
Townend, M. Stewart
Mathematics in sport. —
(Ellis Horwood series in mathematics and its applications)
1. Sports — Mathematics
I. Title
796'.01'51   GV706.8

Library of Congress Card No. 84-6639

ISBN 0-85312-717-4 (Ellis Horwood Limited Library Edn.)
ISBN 0-85312-779-4 (Ellis Horwood Limited Student Edn.)
ISBN 0-470-20082-4 (Halsted Press)

Typeset by Ellis Horwood Limited.
Printed in Great Britain by Unwin Brothers of Woking.

Table of Contents

Foreword. 7
Preface 8
Acknowledgements 11

Chapter 1   RUNNING
           1.1   The mechanics of running. 13
           1.2   A mathematical model of running. 23
           1.3   Hurdling and steeplechase 28

Chapter 2   THROWING
           2.1   Shot put analysis, including treatment of air resistance . . .34
           2.2   Hammer throwing 38
           2.3   The optimum angle of release for shot and hammer 44
           2.4   Discus and javelin 46
           2.5   Basketball shooting 47

Chapter 3   JUMPING
           3.1   The straddle and Fosbury flop high jump techniques 52
           3.2   The pole vault. 58
           3.3   The long jump 66
           3.4   The long jump world record – an analysis 70
           3.5   The triple jump. 73

Chapter 4   FITNESS
           4.1   Isometric endurance. 76
           4.2   How fit are you? (Harvard step test) 81

Chapter 5   MISCELLANEOUS SPORTS
           5.1   Optimum strategy for positioning of oarsmen 88
           5.2   The number of oarsmen in a boat 92

            5.3   Downhill skiing. 94
            5.4   One hundred and eighty! – or less?. 98
            5.5   Ice skating, gymnastics and highboard diving 101

Chapter 6   **SAILING**
            6.1   General discussion of aero- and hydrodynamic
                   phenomena in sailing 108
            6.2   Reynold's number 119
            6.3   Boundary layer 119
            6.4   Winged keels. 121
            6.5   Windsurfing 123
            6.6   Centre of pressure 128
            6.7   Pumping 131
            6.8   Relative velocity 133

Chapter 7   **BALL GAMES**
            7.1   The different possible levels of analysis of ball games . . . 136
            7.2   Elementary collision theory. 136
            7.3   The effects of skidding and spinning 144
            7.4   The effect of the medium through which the
                   ball moves 147
            7.5   Forward passes in rugby football 157
            7.6   The effect of the wind on the motion of a ball 159
            7.7   Cricket versus baseball – which is the more difficult
                   sport to master? 163

Appendix I: BASIC computer program for determining the moment of
                 inertia of a runner's leg about a horizontal axis through
                 the hip. 165

Appendix II: BASIC computer program for determining the length of
                 the throw or long jump for the shot put, hammer throw
                 and long jump events 171

Appendix III: BASIC computer program for determining the optimum
                 angle of projection of the shot, hammer or long jumper
                 and subsequent calculation of the resulting range. 180

Appendix IV: BASIC computer program for determining the success
                 or failure of a basketball free throw. 187

Index 196

Foreword

I very much welcome this new book about links between mathematics and sport. For the mathematician it provides an extremely valuable source of material which has an intrinsic interest level for most people. To a mathematician it shows just how mathematical analysis can be used to explain the mechanics of many sporting events as well as indicating how performance can be improved. Mathematics teachers both at secondary school and in higher education will, I am sure, find this a most valuable source of material which will enrich their teaching of many mathematical topics.

For the sporting enthusiast there is a chance to see just how effective mathematical analysis can be in helping to improve their techniques. Whilst mathematical analysis usually only confirms what intuition tells the expert sportsman, it is nevertheless gratifying to validate one's own instinct.

It is with pleasure I recommend this book to both mathematicians and sportsmen.

David Burghes
University of Exeter

Preface

This book is based on a mathematics course given to Sports Science students at Liverpool Polytechnic, and is intended to show how mathematics can play an important role throughout sport for both explaining known results and determining optimal strategies.

Since the majority of students have some interest in sport, even if only when viewed from an armchair, much of the material has also been used successfully to provide novel, stimulating and interesting applications of mathematics for advanced high school mathematics students and undergraduates in universites and polytechnics from a wide range of disciplines other than Sports Science and Physical Education.

Although exercises are not included at the end of each chapter, there are sufficient questions asked and problems posed throughout the book to make it a valuable source of project ideas. Many of the examples are described with sufficient experimental detail for students to repeat the experiment and gather their own data for analysis. Alternatively, the examples can be used to pre- or post-motivate a lecture topic or to provide the basis of mathematical modelling exercises.

The appendix contains the listings of a suite of interactive BASIC programs with sports applications, together with samples of the output. The lack of computer graphics in this chapter is deliberate because the topic is very machine-dependent. The interested reader could develop the appropriate graphics programs fairly easily and so obtain a much more attractive output to the programs than the author's tables of results.

The sports events discussed in this book have been restricted to those which can be analysed using advanced high school and first-year undergraduate mathematics. Since there is some variation in the syllabus content of the different examining bodies and academic institutions, the mathematical prerequisites for each chapter follow:

Chapter 1 — Running
Slope of the tangent as a measure of rate of change; Simpson's rule; moment

of a force; moment of inertia; parallel axes theorem; elementary integration ($s = \int v\, dt$); Newton's laws of motion; first order ordinary differential equations – variables separable; linear regression.

Chapter 2 – Throwing
Equations of motion under constant acceleration; range of a projectile in a vacuum; roots of a quadratic equation; differentials and their relationship with derivatives; circular motion and central forces; angular momentum; equations of motion for circular motion; principle of conservation of angular momentum; vector product; elementary differentiation of trigonometric functions; determination of maximum and minimum values for functions of one variable.

Chapter 3 – Jumping
Impulse; principle of conservation of linear momentum; location of centre of mass of composite bodies; kinetic and potential energy; principle of conservation or energy; angular momentum; moment of a force; equations of motion in vector form; first order ordinary differential equations – solution by separation of variables; Maclaurin series.

Chapter 4 – Fitness
Use of log-log and semi-log graph paper; least squares line of best fit; correlation coefficient; nomogram; mean and standard deviation; use of t-test as a test of significance.

Chapter 5 – Miscellaneous sports
Resolution of forces; moment of a force; use of log-log graph paper; coefficient of friction; Newton's laws of motion; terminal velocity; first order ordinary differential equations – solution by separation of variables and integrating factors; differentials and their relationship with derivatives; elementary probability for mutually exclusive and independent events; moment of inertia; parallel axes theorem; angular momentum; principle of conservation of angular momentum.

Chapter 6 – Sailing
Bernoulli's theorem; moment of a force; resolution of forces into components; Reynolds number; boundary layer; centre of pressure; double integration; integration by parts; relative velocity.

Chapter 7 – Ball games
Coefficient of restitution; Newton's law of impact; principle of conservation of energy; direct and oblique impacts; principle of conservation of linear momentum; moment of an impulsive blow; spin; frictional force and coefficient of sliding friction; angular acceleration; condition for rolling of a rotating object; Magnus effect; centre of percussion; relative velocity.

Appendices – BASIC programs
The appendices contain a suite of interactive computer programs, written in BASIC, which can be used to investigate the following phenomena, described in the text:

Program 1 – RUNNERLEG–MOI: the moment of inertia of a runner's leg. The program uses a two cylinder model of a leg. The user supplies the runner's body weight and dimensions of the two cylinders. The program computes and outputs the moment of inertia of the runner's leg, about a horizontal axis through the hip, for a range of user-supplied leg positions.

Program 2 – LJTHROWS. This program enables the user to select any of the following three events: shot, hammer and long jump. In response to prompts, the user provides values of the release/take-off velocity, release angle and release height. The program computes the range obtained and outputs the result. The user can repeat the input and thus perform a sensitivity analysis of the event.

Program 3 – OPTIRELANGLE. The optimum angle of release for trajectory problems. In response to prompts for values of the release velocity and release height the program computes the optimum angle of release for the projectile. This value is then used to compute and output the range resulting from use of this angle of release. For comparison purposes, the current world records are also given for the events considered.

Program 4 – B/BALLFREETHROW: basketball free throws. For user input of release velocity and release height of the basketball the program first computes the two angles of projection consistent with the centre of the ball passing through the centre of the hoop. Both these angles of projection are then tested to determine whether either produces an angle of entry (β) such that

$$\beta > 33.14°,$$

as required by the geometrical consideration of the ball's entry to the hoop. The user can repeat the experiment for different values of release velocity and release height. Whatever the outcome of the 'throw' a suitable message is printed out for the user.

In conclusion I should like to record my thanks to the many people whose assistance and advice were invaluable in the preparation of this book – in particular many students at Liverpool Polytechnic whose comments and work have contributed to this book, Dr. Thomas Reilly of Liverpool Polytechnic for many helpful discussions, Mrs. Joyce Yoxon for her production of typed order from chaos and my wife, Lesley, whose patience made the book possible.

Acknowledgements

The author wishes to express his gratitude to the following authors and publishers who have generously permitted use of their materials.

Chapter 1.   §1.2 Based on a communication from Professor D. N. Burghes, University of Exeter.

Keller, J. B. 'Optimal Velocity in a Race', *American Mathematical Monthly,* Vol. 81 (1974).

Chapter 2.   Fig. 2.4 reproduced, with permission, from *Hammer Throwing* by Howard Payne, an A.A.A. publication (1969).

Chapter 3.   Figs. 3.1, 3.3, 3.4 reproduced, with permission, from 'Is the Fosbury Flop A Mechanical Success?' by E. A. Trowbridge. Published in *Mathematical Spectrum*, Vol. 12, No. 2 (1979/1980).

Figure 3.8 Hand hold figure reproduced, with permission, from *Pole Vault* by Alan Neuff, a B.A.A.B. publication (1975).

§3.4 Based on a communication from Professor D. N. Burghes, University of Exeter.

Chapter 4.   Fig. 4.4 Dubois Body Surface Chart: Nomograph. Copyright 1920 by W. M. Boothby and R. B. Sandiford, Mayo Clinic, Rochester, Minn., USA.

Table 4.1 Calculation of Girls Physical Efficiency Index: Modified Harvard Step Test. Originally published in 'A Functional Fitness Test for High School Girls' by L. Brouha and J. R. Gallagher, *Journal of Health and Physical Education,* Vol. 15, No. 10 (1943).

Chapter 5.   §5.1 Based on 'Oar Arrangements in Rowing Eights' by M. N. Brearley.
§5.2 Based on a section of 'Mechanical Aspects of Athletics' by J. B. Keller.

Both published in *Optimal Strategies in Sports* (Studies in Management Science and Systems 5), edited by S. P. Ladany and R. E. Machol, North Holland Publishing Company, Amsterdam (1977).

The computer programs contained in this book are offered in the form of convenient disks. The software is substantially the same as the listings in the book.

It is important to understand that, although the programs in this book have been carefully tested, it is the user's responsibility to ensure normal safety precautions are exercised when the programs are applied to practical problems.

The disks are available from the publisher: Ellis Horwood Limited, Market Cross House, Cooper Street, Chichester, West Sussex PO19 1EB, England.

1

Running

1.1 THE MECHANICS OF RUNNING

In all running events the objective is to cover a given distance in as short a time as possible relative to the opposition. This time is determined by the athlete's speed which in turn depends on two quantities

(i) the stride length,
(ii) the stride frequency.

Obviously the values of these two quantities depend upon the nature of the event (a sprinter has a much longer stride than a marathoner). Examination of the performances of male sprinters, with 100 m times in the range 10 s to 11.5 s, has shown that there is a close relationship between the athlete's anthropological parameters of height and leg length and his stride length and frequency. On average it was found that

$$\text{stride length} = \begin{cases} 1.14 \times \text{height} \\ 2.11 \times \text{leg length} \end{cases}$$

and that the value of the numerical factors tended to increase as the quality of the athlete increased.

Once the starting pistol has been fired the athlete's main concern is to accelerate to his maximum speed as quickly as possible and then to maintain it for as long as possible. It will be appreciated that here we refer exclusively to sprint events (100 m, 200 m and 400 m) for which the duration is so short that the question of tactics is not relevant.

For the middle- and long-distance events the athletes use a standing start but for the sprints (100 m, 200 m and 400 m) the majority of athletes employ a start technique which uses starting blocks. There are several such techniques and they are classified by the toe-to-toe distance, measured between the feet when the athlete is in the set position in the blocks, see Fig. 1.1.

Fig. 1.1 — Toe-to-toe distance.

The names of the three techniques together with typical values of the toe-to-toe distances for college athletes are:

(i) the bullet start, toe-to-toe distance 0.28 m approximately,
(ii) the medium start, toe-to-toe distance in the range 0.4 m − 0.53 m approximately,
(iii) the elongated start, toe-to-toe distance in the range 0.61 m − 0.71 m approximately.

The toe-to-toe distances for younger athletes would generally be less than the figures quoted here.

It is of interest to assess the relative merits of the different techniques. The data presented in Table 1.1 relate to a top-class female college sprinter. The method by which the data were obtained is described so that you can repeat the experiment with a sprinter of your acquaintance.

The sprinter was timed at different distances during the first four seconds of the event, with more attention given to the first few metres since it is during this phase that the athlete's acceleration is greatest. Four seconds was selected since is was considered that after that time the sprinter was running with her full stride length and frequency. The distance—time data obtained were then smoothed graphically and the velocity determined at various times by measuring the slope of the tangent, see Fig. 1.2.

Table 1.1 reveals some interesting features about the start techniques. It can be seen that initially the highest velocities are obtained with the bullet start which means that with this technique the blocks are cleared fastest. At a later stage of the four-second interval the highest velocities now correspond to the medium start. Does this indicate that an athlete using this technique would now be further down the track than if the bullet start had been used?

The actual distance travelled during the first four seconds using each of the start techniques can be determined from the velocity—time data using Simpson's rule to evaluate the integral

$$\int_0^4 v \, dt.$$

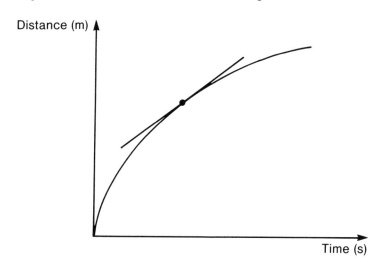

Distance (m)

Time (s)

Fig. 1.2 – Distance–time graph for sprinter. Instantaneous velocity given by slope of tangent.

Table 1.1
Velocity–time data for female sprinter.

| Time (s) | Velocity (ms^{-1}) | | |
	Medium	Bullet	Elongated
0.0	0	0	0
0.5	1.52	2.56	1.40
1.0	2.87	3.54	2.56
1.5	3.90	3.96	3.41
2.0	4.69	4.33	4.08
2.5	5.24	4.69	4.57
3.0	5.67	5.12	4.94
3.5	6.10	5.55	5.30
4.0	6.46	5.91	5.58

The results are:

medium start:	distance travelled = 16.66 m
bullet start:	distance travelled = 16.55 m
elongated start:	distance travelled = 14.58 m

which indicate that, for this sprinter, the medium start technique is the best to use. It must be emphasized that this conclusion could vary with the individual athlete although it is true to say that the majority of sprinters do use a medium start. You may wonder why the starts were not assessed by simply measuring how far the athlete travelled during the phase examined. This was not done since after four seconds of the event the athlete is travelling quite quickly (approximately $7 \, \text{ms}^{-1}$) and it would have been very difficult to accurately mark the spot on the ground corresponding to four seconds.

In some events, such as the 200 m and 400 m, the athletes start on a bend. While the athlete is negotiating the bend the ground exerts a horizontal force against the foot which acts inwards towards the centre of the arc of the bend. This has the undesirable effect of rotating the athlete outwards and he compensates for this by 'leaning into the bend' so that the moment about his centre of mass of the vertical ground reaction will provide a countering moment to the centripetal force. If the athlete is running very fast or if the radius of the bend is small (as is often the case with indoor tracks) the ground is no longer able to to provide a sufficiently large centripetal force. Unless alternative provisions are made the athlete either has to slow for the bends or risk an accident. To avoid this, indoor tracks are built with banked bends. This enables the component of the athletes weight which acts down the slope to contribute to the centripetal force so reducing, or even eliminating, the need for an inward lean.

Immediately after the start there is a period during which the athlete accelerates to his maximum speed. Just as an automobile will not accelerate rapidly if started in too high a gear neither will an athlete. Instead the athlete must begin with a relatively short stride and high stride frequency. As the speed increases (and the acceleration decreases) the stride length gets longer until when maximum speed has been reached (zero acceleration) the stride length has increased to its maximum value. During this acceleration phase, the orientation of the athlete's body also changes. At the start the athlete is crouched low over the start line or set in the starting blocks. This position is adopted so that when the starting pistol is fired the driving action of the leg has a large horizontal component to give the athlete a large horizontal acceleration. Fig. 1.3 shows that H, the horizontal component of the driving force, tends to rotate the athlete backwards about the centre of mass, G. To overcome this rotation, the athlete leans well forward in order to reduce the moment of the horizontal reaction and increase the counteracting effect of the vertical reaction V. After a few strides the horizontal speed of the athlete will have increased considerably and he will no longer be able to exert the same large horizontal force. In order to prevent a forward rotation due to the vertical reaction the athlete raises his trunk so reducing the moment of the vertical reaction. These adjustments of the body orientation continue until the athlete reaches his maximum speed at which point the horizontal force exerted against the ground is just sufficient to counteract the retarding effect of the air resistance, R. Nevertheless it is still necessary for the athlete to counter the small backward rotating effects of the air resistance and the horizontal reaction. If the athlete does not do this, the body will eventually rotate into a

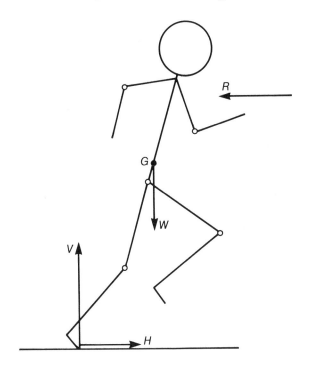

Fig. 1.3 – Body inclination is determined by the forces acting on it.

position from which it is impossible to apply sufficient horizontal force to maintain maximum speed. It is for this reason that elite sprinters exhibit a forward inclination of the trunk even when running at maximum speed.

Throughout the duration of any running event the leg action is cyclical with the cycle divided into three phases:

(i) the support phase — defined as the stage from the landing of the foot to the instant when the body's centre of mass passes ahead of the foot's landing position,

(ii) the drive phase — which begins at the end of the support phase and finishes as the foot leaves the ground,

(iii) the recovery phase — the interval during which the foot is off the ground and is being moved to its next contact with the ground.

The beginning of the support phase occurs as the foot lands on the ground at which time it could be moving forwards, vertically downwards or backwards relative to the direction in which the athlete is running. If the foot is moving forwards on landing then the reaction of the ground will include a backwards horizontal force which retards the athlete. If the foot is moving vertically downwards on landing then there is no effect on the horizontal motion of the athlete while if the foot is moving backwards on landing then the ground reaction will include a forwards horizontal component which increases the athlete's velocity. In practice there is always some retarding effect as the foot makes contact with the ground.

During the drive phase the athlete thrusts downwards and backwards against the ground. The effect of this is to project the athlete upwards and forwards into the next stride. Once the athlete breaks contact with the ground he can be considered as a projectile. The trajectory of the centre of mass is then governed by many features such as its height above ground level at take-off, the velocity components at take-off and air resistance effects. The take-off velocity has by far the greatest effect on the length of the stride. It is established in the section on shot putting that the range is proportional to the square of the release velocity. Since the take-off velocity of the runner has a large horizontal component and a small vertical component (unlike high jumping) then the resultant velocity is almost horizontal. Consequently the parabolic trajectory will be very flat. This is apparent if you watch an athlete who is running in a stadium against a background of a horizontal line for it is seen that the head maintains approximately the same horizontal level throughout the run, excluding the start phase.

During the recovery phase the foot is brought forward from behind the body to the point on the ground at which contact is next made. Once the foot breaks contact with the ground the leg bends sharply at the knee and the foot is raised to a position close to and underneath the buttocks. The effect of this is to reduce the moment of inertia of the limb relative to a transverse axis through the hips thus enabling the leg to rotate forwards more quickly about this axis than would be the case if the leg was not sharply bent (remember both that angular momentum $= Iw$ and the principle of conservation of angular momentum).

The extent to which the leg is bent is one of the distinguishing features of the specific leg action of sprinters and middle- and long-distance runners. Long-distance runners, notably marathoners, do not raise their feet to the same extent as sprinters. Thus the moment of inertia of their legs about the hips is greater than for a sprinter and consequently the angular velocity is less. It thus takes longer for the leg to move through to start the running cycle again, as is to be expected since they are not running so fast. Fig. 1.4 shows a sequence of tracings taken from a film of a runner's leg during a stride. The upper leg and combined lower leg and foot can each be modelled as a circular cylinder, typically with the following dimensions

uper leg: mass $= 0.137 \times$ mass of athlete, radius $= 0.07$ m, length $= 0.45$ m, lower leg and foot: mass $= 0.06 \times$ mass of athlete, radius $= 0.05$ m,
             length $= 0.50$ m.

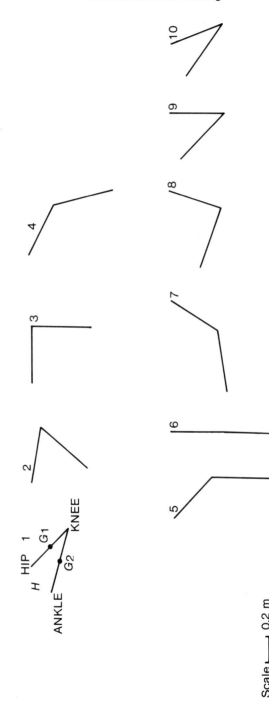

Fig. 1.4(i) – Sequence of positions of one leg for a sprinter.

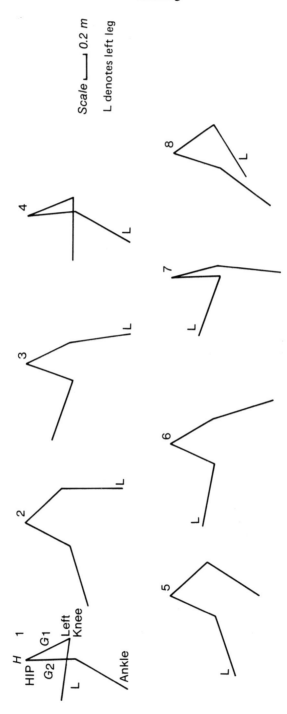

Fig. 1.4(ii) — Sequence of leg positions for middle-distance runner.

The moment of inertia of the complete limb about the transverse axis through the hip can then be determined by using the parallel axes theorem together with the result that for a cylinder of mass m, radius a and length h the moment of inertia I about an axis through its centre and perpendicular to the length of the cylinder is given by

$$I = m\left(\frac{a^2}{4} + \frac{h^2}{12}\right).$$

Referring to Fig. 1.4(i) position 1 in the case of an athlete who weighs 73 kg

$$\text{upper leg, } I_{G_1} = 0.137 \times 73 \left(\frac{0.07^2}{4} + \frac{0.45^2}{12}\right) = 0.181 \text{ kgm}^2,$$

$$\text{lower leg and foot, } I_{G_2} = 0.06 \times 73 \left(\frac{0.05^2}{4} + \frac{0.5^2}{12}\right) = 0.094 \text{ kgm}^2.$$

Hence by the parallel axes theorem the moment of inertia of the whole limb about the transverse axis through the hips is

$$\begin{aligned}
I_H &= 0.181 + 0.137 \times 73 \times (0.225)^2 + 0.094 + 0.06 \times 73 \times HG_2^2 \\
&= 0.181 + \qquad 0.506 \qquad + 0.094 + 0.06 \times 73 \times (0.24)^2. \\
&= 1.033 \text{ kgm}^2
\end{aligned}$$

Appendix I contains a BASIC computer program which can be used to perform the above calculation for each of the limb positions shown in Fig. 1.4 using the scale provided to determine the various values of the length HG_2.

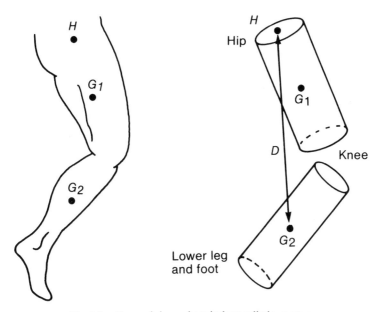

Fig. 1.5 — Runner's leg and equivalent cylinder system.

The results are shown in Fig. 1.6 from which it is apparent that the moment of inertia of the whole limb varies considerably with the position adopted.

The moment of inertia is least when the mass of the limb is concentrated close to the axis of rotation and increases throughout the stride to reach a maximum when the leg is fully extended. Since angular momentum = Iw and is constant throughout the leg motion, then the angular velocity of the leg is greatest when the leg is bent up close to the buttocks and least when the leg is fully extended. Thus the leg can be brought forwards more rapidly for the next stride if it is bent acutely at the knee.

The arms too have their part to play in running. As the right knee is carried forward and upward during the recovery phase of the right leg cycle the hips rotate anticlockwise (viewed from above). This rotation ceases as the knee reaches its high point. The right leg then descends to the ground and the left leg begins to move forwards and upwards causing a clockwise rotation of the hips. These rotations would have a detrimental effect on the athlete's stability if left unchecked. The arms provide the counteraction for as the right leg moves forwards and upwards (to cause an anticlockwise rotation) the left arm is driven forwards and upwards to cause an opposite clockwise rotation. Some athletes also tend to swing the shoulders excessively in order to counteract the

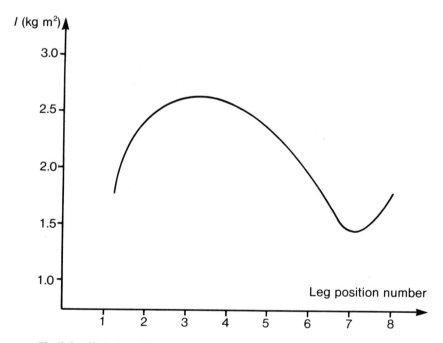

Fig. 1.6 – Variation with leg position of the moment of inertia of the complete leg about a horizontal axis through the hips for a middle-distance runner.

hip rotation. The rotation of the shoulders is, however, relatively slow and the hip rotation is best counteracted by a vigorous arm action. The vigour and range of the arm action varies according to the event; it is vigorous and of considerable amplitude for sprinters while for marathoners it is less in both these respects.

1.2 A MATHEMATICAL MODEL OF RUNNING

Whenever an attempt is made to produce a mathematical model of a system, the first step is to decide upon the relevant variables. In running events the athlete's velocity is obviously of paramount importance. If the time dependent velocity of an athlete is $v(t)$ and a distance D is covered in time τ then from the integral calculus

$$D = \int_0^\tau v(t)\, dt. \tag{1.1}$$

Although in practice the winning athlete selects a function $v(t)$ which enables him to beat his opponents, we shall assume that he tries to run the race in the least time possible. While such an assumption is valid for the sprint events it is certainly not valid for middle- and long-distance events in which tactical ability is almost as important as running ability. Some information about the velocity $v(t)$ can be obtained from consideration of the equation of motion of the athlete. Suppose the athlete of mass m exerts a propulsive force $F(t)$ per unit mass and experiences resistive forces of amount R per unit mass then application of Newton's second law of motion gives:

$$m\,\frac{dv}{dt} = mF(t) - mR.$$

In many situations the resistance force R experienced by a body is found experimentally to be proportional to the first or second power of the velocity. The resistance is proportional to the square of the velocity if the body is streamlined, such as a sledge or downhill skier, whereas if the body is more blunt in shape the resistance is proportional to the first power of the velocity. A runner certainly comes in the latter category and thus we shall assume

$$R \propto v$$

so that

$$R = kv.$$

The equation of motion then becomes

$$\frac{dv}{dt} = F(t) - kv. \tag{1.2}$$

This is a first order differential equation and in order to obtain its solution we shall need an initial condition which may be obtained from the fact that the athlete starts from rest,

$$v(0) = 0. \tag{1.3}$$

The propulsive force $F(t)$ is supplied by the athlete. Although the athlete will be unaware of the precise mathematical nature of this force, one thing about it is certain; the physiological limitations of each athlete determine a maximum propulsive force which that athlete cannot exceed. If this value is denoted by F^* then

$$F(t) \leqslant F^* \tag{1.4}$$

The fact that locomotion can take place at all is due to the body's ability to absorb into the blood the oxygen contained in the inspired air and then to transport it to the muscles required for locomotion. The extent to which this oxygen transport system is developed varies from one athlete to another. If $E(t)$ denotes the amount of oxygen available in the muscles per unit mass of body at time t then we can write

$$\frac{\mathrm{d}E}{\mathrm{d}t} = S - Fv, \tag{1.5}$$

where S is the rate of oxygen supply in excess of that required in the non-running state and Fv is the rate of use of energy calculated from the propulsive force.

Initially a certain amount of oxygen is available so

$$E(0) = E_0, \text{ a constant}, \tag{1.6}$$

and throughout the event we must obviously satisfy the inequality

$$E(t) \geqslant 0. \tag{1.7}$$

Although the problem of minimizing τ subject to the above conditions, (1.3) and (1.6), and constraints (1.1), (1.4) and (1.7), is beyond the scope of this book (it is a sophisticated problem in optimisation and the interested reader is referred to Keller (1974)) it can be brought within the scope of this book if the sprints and the longer events are considered separately.

The Sprints
For these events (the 100 m, 200 m and 400 m) it is assumed that the athlete's propulsive force takes its maximum value throughout the duration of the event, i.e. $F(t) = F^*$. The equation of motion (1.2) then becomes

$$\frac{\mathrm{d}v}{\mathrm{d}t} = F^* - kv,$$

which is to be solved subject to $v(0) = 0$.

Separating the variables and integrating then gives

$$\int_0^v \frac{dv}{F^* - kv} = \int_0^t dt,$$

whence

$$v(t) = \frac{F^*}{k} (1 - e^{-kt}) .$$

This expression for $v(t)$ is now substituted into equation (1.1) to give

$$D = \frac{F^*}{k} \int_0^\tau (1 - e^{-kt}) dt$$

i.e.

$$D = \frac{F^*}{k} [\tau - \frac{1}{k}(1 - e^{-k\tau})] . \tag{1.8}$$

Equation (1.8) expresses the relationship between the distance D of a sprint event and τ the time taken on the assumption that the athlete exerts the maximum possible propulsive force throughout the event. The validity of the result should now be checked and this poses something of a problem for the values of F^* and k are unknown. In order to determine them we are forced to use two of our three sprint results which only leaves one sprint result with which to validate equation (1.8). This is hardly adequate!

In order to validate the model more rigorously the following experiment was performed in order to obtain distance–time data at numerous intermediate stages.

A trained college sprinter performed a 100 m sprint. Fellow students each equipped with a stop-watch, were placed at intervals down the length of the track. They were asked to start their stopwatches as the starting pistol was fired and to stop it as the sprinter passed directly in front of them. In this way a set of distance–time data was obtained. The instantaneous velocity values were obtained by smoothing the distance–time curve and then determining the slope of the tangent at a selection of points on the curve. (If you have access to a set of photocells you will be able to determine the velocity values much more accurately than the foregoing procedure.) The results enabled a velocity–time curve to be drawn. It too was smoothed and the slope of the tangents determined at a selection of points to give a set of acceleration values. The results obtained by the author are given in Table 1.2. If you repeat the exercise using the given distance–time data you will probably find that your results are slightly different. This is because both the graphical smoothing and the estimation of the tangents are subjective processes. Numerical procedures, which remove this subjectivity, are available for determining the values of the acceleration from the values of the displacement although their use is beyond the scope of this book.

The values of F^* and k can be estimated from the equation of motion (1.2),

$$a = F^* - kv.$$

Table 1.2

Distance–time data for 100 m sprint. Values of velocity and acceleration
have been determined from the slope of tangents.

Elapsed time t(s)	Distance d(m)	Velocity v(ms^{-1})	Acceleration a(ms^{-2})
0	0	0	
1	2.5	5.3	2.0
2	9.5	6.8	
3	19.0	7.7	0.8
4	27.5	8.4	
5	37.5	8.95	0.55
6	45.0	9.4	
7	52.0	9.5	0.125
8	60.0	9.6	
9	70.5	9.6	0
10	78.0	9.6	
11	87.0	9.6	
12	94.5	9.55	−0.1
12.6	100.0	9.5	

Fig. 1.7 shows a graph of acceleration plotted against velocity. The value of
F^* corresponds to the intercept of the graph and the value of $-k$ corresponds to
the slope of the graph. Although it is possible to fit a straight line through the
points and estimate the best fit by eye the values given in Fig. 1.7 were obtained
using a linear regression technique. This enabled the correlation coefficient, r, to
be determined. This coefficient is a measure of how well the line fits the data,
the nearer the value of $|r|$ is to 1 the better the fit. It can thus be seen that the
fit is 'very good' indicating the validity of the original assertion that sprinters
exert their maximum propulsive force throughout the duration of the event.

Table 1.3 provides a comparison between the theoretical distance travelled by
the sprinter in a time t s, determined from equation (1.8), and the actual distance
travelled.

Middle- and long-distance events
The assumption made with these events is that the velocity of the athlete is
constant throughout the event. This means that the initial phase of acceleration
after the start has been neglected as have the tactical considerations which so

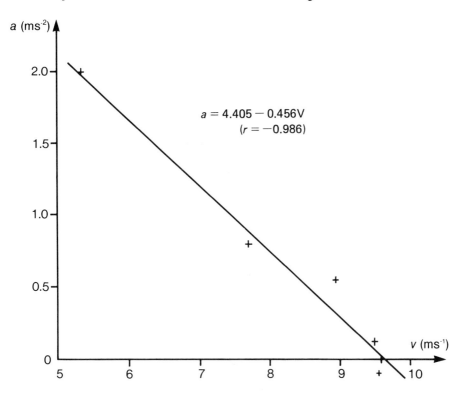

Fig. 1.7 – Graph of acceleration versus velocity for 100 m sprinter.

Table 1.3
Comparison of actual and theoretical distances travelled by a 100 m sprinter
in different times t s.

t(s)	Actual distance travelled (m)	Theoretical distance travelled (m)	Difference (m)
1	2.50	1.90	−0.60
3	19.0	13.19	−5.81
5	37.5	29.28	−8.22
7	52.0	47.31	−4.69
9	70.5	66.10	−4.40
12	94.5	94.82	+0.32
12.6	100.0	100.60	+0.60

often characterize these longer events. Since the velocity is constant then $dv/dt = 0$ and the equation of motion (1.2) implies

$$v = \frac{1}{k} F(t).$$

Suppose further that at the end of the race the athlete has no oxygen left in the muscles then

$$E(\tau) = 0.$$

Considering the condition of some athletes at the end of a hard 1500 m, 10 000 m or marathon this is not an unreasonable assumption! Since v is constant then equation (1.5) can be easily integrated to give

$$\int_{E_0}^{0} dE = \int_{0}^{\tau} (S - Fv)\, dt,$$

i.e.

$$0 - E_0 = \int_{0}^{\tau} (S - kv^2)\, dt$$
$$= (S - kv^2)\tau$$

so

$$v^2 = \frac{1}{k} (S + \frac{E_0}{\tau}).$$

Finally the expression for v is substituted into equation (1.1) to give

$$D = \int_{0}^{\tau} \sqrt{\left\{ \frac{1}{k} (S + \frac{E_0}{\tau}) \right\}}\, dt,$$

i.e.

$$D = \tau^2 \cdot \frac{S}{k} + \tau \cdot \frac{E_0}{k}. \tag{1.9}$$

Equation (1.9) expresses the relationship between the distance D of a non-sprint event and the time taken τ on the assumption that the athlete maintains a constant velocity throughout the event. Once again validation of equation (1.9) presents a problem. Since there are four non-sprint track events (the 800 m, 1500 m, 5000 m and 10 000 m) and the data for two of them are needed to estimate the values of S/k and E_0/k in equation (1.9) this only leaves two pairs of data with which to validate the model. As before, this is hardly sufficient. What is needed are some displacement values at intermediate times. Perhaps you can collect some and validate the above model as was done for the sprints?

1.3 HURDLING AND STEEPLECHASE

There is a total of four different hurdles events each requiring the athlete to clear ten hurdles.

(i) 110 m hurdles for men, hurdle height 1.067 m,
(ii) 100 m hurdles for women, hurdle height 0.84 m,
(iii) 200 m hurdles for men and women, hurdle height 0.762 m,
(iv) 400 m hurdles for men and women, hurdle height 0.914 m and 0.76 m respectively.

In each event the athlete must attempt to clear each hurdle while preserving the normal running action as much as possible. Hurdling is not simply a matter of jumping over a barrier; if an unnecessary amount of time is spent in the air then time is being wasted since a propulsive force can only be exerted while in contact with the ground. For example the difference between the times recorded by the world class 110 m hurdlers and sprinters is less than two seconds illustrating how little time an efficient hurdler spends in the air.

In the men's 110 m hurdles event the distance to the first hurdle is 13.72 m, the distance between each of the hurdles is 9.14 m and the distance from the last hurdle to the finish is 14.02 m. Since the hurdles are placed in specific positions it is essential for the athlete to adapt his running action to take account of this. In particular it is necessary for the athlete to adopt an upright position sooner than in an ordinary sprint in order to prepare for the take-off over the first hurdle. Also, in order to obtain the correct stride pattern for take-off at the first hurdle the athlete may need to move the starting blocks further back.

Take-off
This part of the action is almost identical to a normal sprinting stride. As soon as the take-off foot has landed at the completion of the last stride before the hurdle, the other foot (called the lead foot) is brought up close to and underneath the buttock. Next, with the lead leg bent at the knee (to reduce its moment of inertia and so speed up the rotation about the hips) the lead knee is swung forwards and upwards. As the knee reaches the limit of this movement the momentum is transferred to the lower leg causing the leading leg to eventually become almost straight. (This flicking up of the lower leg has a voluntary as well as a mechanical aspect and is one of the aspects of hurdling technique which coaches find most difficult to instill in an athlete.) This tends to rotate the athlete backwards and is countered by the hurdler moving his trunk forward and downward.

The distance from the hurdle at which the athlete takes off depends on various factors such as approach speed, height of athlete, leg length and speed of leading leg and so varies from one athlete to another but an average figure is 2.13 m. Similarly the average value of the distance of the foot from the hurdle on landing is 1.22 m. In general, the faster the athlete is travelling the further back from the hurdle is the take-off point. Since the athlete will be building up speed over the first few hurdles and slowing down over the last few (owing to the effects of fatigue) it follows that the take-off distance may vary throughout the event. For this reason only an average figure was quoted.

Clearance

Once the athlete has left the ground the only forces acting are gravity and air resistance. Since time in the air corresponds to time wasted it is desirable for the athlete to clear the hurdle by as small an amount as possible consistent with safety and a controlled landing. This puts the athlete back in contact with the ground as soon as possible and enables the next driving phase to begin. The height to which the athlete's centre of mass is raised is determined solely by the vertical component of the take-off velocity and thus an excessivley large value should be avoided since this will only serve to raise the centre of mass unnecessarily high. During the clearance phase the athlete also experiences the air resistance effects which serve to reduce the horizontal component of velocity. This effect is reduced to a certain extent by the reduction in frontal area of the athlete caused by the forward lean of the trunk mentioned above in the takeoff section. The forward lean also has the added advantage that it lowers the athlete's centre of mass and thus reduces the height to which the centre of mass must be raised to clear the hurdle.

As soon as the knee of the leading leg crosses the hurdle, the backward and downward action of the lead leg begins and the trunk is raised towards the vertical in preparation for the landing and the start of the next drive phase. Since the athlete only just clears the hurdle, the trailing leg has to be lifted outward so that it passes horizontally over the hurdle. In all other respects its action is identical to that of the trailing leg in sprinting.

Landing

When the hurdler lands from the clearance phase the body is almost erect. From this position he then drives vigorously into his next running stride. The trailing leg helps enormously in this drive since as it is returned to a vertical plane it is driven forwards and upwards to put the athlete into a normal sprinting attitude.

If the foot on which the athlete lands is too far ahead of the vertical through the body's centre of mass then the athlete will experience a braking effect. Consequently it is recommended in the coaching manuals that the landing foot should be positioned below the body's centre of mass.

From this position the athlete moves to the next take-off position in three strides and the cycle is repeated. It has already been noted that the running action of middle- and long-distance runners is simply a less vigorous version of the sprinter's actions. The same may be said of the longer sprint events vis-a-vis the 110 m hurdles race.

In the 400 m hurdles event the distance to the first hurdle is 45 m, the distance between the hurdles is 35 m and the final run-in distance is 40 m. The hurdles are lower than in the 110 m event so it is easier for the athlete to maintain a smooth running style over them.

The major problem faced by a 400 m hurdler is how many strides to use between the hurdles. The number chosen must be consistent with the athlete's normal stride length since any attempt to over- or under-reach will certainly reduce his speed. Unless the athlete can hurdle from either foot it will be necessary to use an odd number of strides between hurdles. Finally it is inevitable that in the later stages of the event the stride length will diminish due to the onset of fatigue and the effect of cornering.

Safety in Hurdling.
In any hurdling event there is a chance that an athlete will make contact with one, or more, hurdles. Provided that the hurdles have been constructed in accordance with the regulations laid down by the athletics authorities, see Fig. 1.8, a competitor may knock down any number of hurdles without disqualification. There is no advantage to be had by simply knocking down all the hurdles since the impacts have considerable retarding and destabilizing effects.

While it is undesirable for a hurdle to overturn if an athlete merely 'brushes' against it, it is imperative that it overturns if the athlete hits it hard, perhaps because of an incorrect take-off. If it did not overturn in such circumstances there would be considerable risk of serious injury to the athlete, since a hurdle weighs at least 10 kg. On the other hand it must not overturn too easily since this would mean it could easily be blown over by a strong wind.

Figure 1.8 shows the dimensions of an approved hurdle. In order to be termed 'approved' the moveable weights must be positioned so that the hurdle will not overturn unless the magnitude of the horizontal force F kg, applied at the centre of the top bar, lies in the range

$$3.6 \leqslant F < 4.0.$$

It is necessary for the weights on the horizontal leg of the hurdle to be moveable since the height of the hurdle varies with the race distance and the sex and age of the competitors. Consequently if we take moments about the bottom crossbar of the hurdle the moment of force F can vary in value thus requiring the moveable weight to be set in different positions to maintain equilibrium.

Steeplechase
This event, run over a distance of 1500 m to 3000 m depending upon the age of the competitors, is physically very demanding since it requires not only the endurance of a runner but also the skills of a hurdler.

The rules stipulate that there must be five obstacles per lap, including a water jump, making a total of thirty-five barriers in all. Unlike the hurdles used in the hurdles races those used in the steeplechase are of a much more substantial construction. They must be capable of supporting the weight of an athlete since it is permitted for the athletes to step on them.

Since the barriers are lower (0.914 m) and a steeplechaser runs more slowly than a pure hurdler then the steeplechaser's hurdling technique will be less

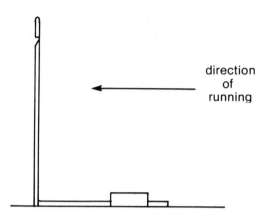

direction
of
running

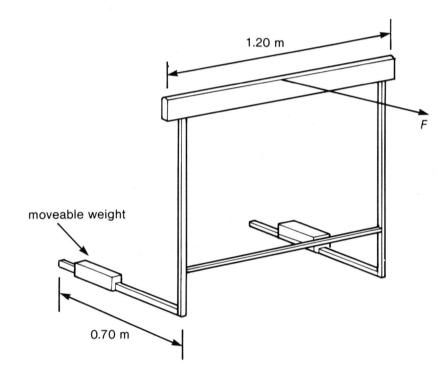

1.20 m

F

moveable weight

0.70 m

Fig. 1.8 – Approved hurdle.

forceful. In particular his take-off velocity will be less and so he will cover less horizontal distance while crossing each barrier. The barriers can be hurdled in the usual way or they can be stepped on with one foot. Many athletes resort to the latter technique once they become affected by fatigue.

The water jump itself is 3.66 m wide (measured in the direction of running) and tapers in depth from 0.76 m at the barrier to 0 m on exit. Since the athletes approach this barrier relatively slowly (certainly more slowly than a long jumper approaches the take-off board) it is impossible for them to clear both the barrier and the water using a hurdling technique. Instead, the take-off is adapted so that the athlete first lands with one foot on the top bar of the hurdle and from this position then drives himself off over the water. Despite this assistance, the majority of steeplechasers still do not possess sufficient momentum to clear the water completely. Instead they land with one foot in the water from which point they continue their running action to regain the track.

2

Throwing

2.1 SHOT PUT ANALYSIS, INCLUDING TREATMENT OF AIR RESISTANCE

The well-known formula $R = \dfrac{V^2 \sin 2\alpha}{g}$ for the range of an object projected with an initial velocity V at an angle α to the horizontal only applies when the points of release and landing are on the same horizontal level. Consequently, the fact that the optimum angle of release is $45°$ does not apply in the case of the shot put since in this event observation shows that the shot is released from a height of between about 2 m and 2.4 m above the ground. Further analysis shows that good-class shot putters achieve a release velocity of the shot of some 13.7 ms^{-1} and a release angle in the range $40°$ to $42°$ to the horizontal. Ideally, when the shot leaves the hand it should be ahead of the stop board on the front of the throwing circle. In fact very few throwers achieve this and so in this chapter the release position of the shot is assumed to be vertically above the stop board.

The problem to be solved is therefore to obtain an expression for the range R of a shot when it is projected from a point at height h above the ground with an initial velocity V at an angle α to the horizontal. The position of the centre of the shot at the moment of release is selected as the origin of coordinates so that the situation is represented by Fig. 2.1.

If the effects of air resistance are ignored, the elementary equations relating to motion under a constant acceleration can be applied. Horizontally, the shot has no acceleration and therefore, after t seconds

$$x = (V \cos \alpha) t. \tag{2.1}$$

In the vertical direction, the shot experiences only the acceleration due to gravity so that

$$y = (V \sin \alpha) t - \frac{1}{2} g t^2. \tag{2.2}$$

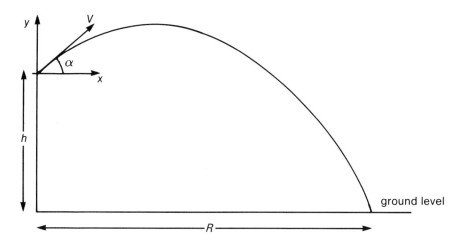

Fig. 2.1 – Notation used in shot put analysis.

The time at which the shot reaches the ground is given by equation (2.2) with $y = -h$ whence

$$gt^2 - 2(V \sin \alpha)t - 2h = 0$$

so that

$$t = \frac{2V \sin \alpha \pm \sqrt{(4V^2 \sin^2 \alpha + 8gh)}}{2g}.$$

Since $\sqrt{(4V^2 \sin^2 \alpha + 8gh)} > 2V \sin \alpha$ it is only sensible to accept the positive root in the above expression, the negative root gives a negative time!

The value obtained for t is then substituted into equation (2.1) to give the range of the throw as

$$R = \frac{V^2 \cos \alpha}{g} \left\{ \sin \alpha + \sqrt{\left(\sin^2 \alpha + \frac{2gh}{V^2}\right)} \right\}. \tag{2.3}$$

In order to see whether this equation predicts a sensible value for the range of a shot put, we can insert some numerical values. The following table gives the range of values of V, α and h for competent senior athletes.

Parameter	Range of Values
V	$10\text{--}14 \text{ ms}^{-1}$
α	$40°\text{--}45°$
h	$1.8\text{--}2.5 \text{ m}$

Using values of $V = 13.7 \text{ ms}^{-1}$, $\alpha = 40°$ and $h = 2.25$ m, together with $g = 9.81$ ms^{-2}, gives the range as $R = 21.22$ m.

Obviously, the values of the above parameters vary from one athlete to another. For example it has already been mentioned that h varies from about 2 m to 2.4 m. If it is assumed that the release velocity and release angle are kept fixed at 13.7 ms^{-1} and 40° then these extremes for h yield the ranges 20.98 m and 21.36 m respectively, illustrating the adage that 'a good big 'un will always beat a good little 'un'.

Appendix II contains a BASIC computer program which you can use not only to calculate the range of a throw for given values of V, α and h but also to investigate how the range varies as any one of these parameters is varied. You will find the most dramatic changes in the range occur when V is varied; can you deduce why?

Since the current world record is 22.15 m we can see that the above formula, although it ignores the effects of air resistance, is valuable for predicting the range of a throw. This is very fortunate because the inclusion of air resistance effects complicates matters considerably as the following shows.

In order to make the analysis realistic, it is necessary to include an air resistance term in the equations of motion.

There is considerable experimental evidence to suggest that for a sphere having the size and speed of a shot the air resistance force D is proportional to the square of the speed V of the shot, i.e.

$$D \propto V^2.$$

The constant of proportionality has been found experimentally to be $0.2 \, d^2$ where d m is the diameter of the shot. For the shot used by senior male athletes $d = 0.15$ m so that

$$D = 0.2 \times 0.15^2 \times V^2 = 0.0045 \, V^2.$$

The air resistance force acts, of course, in the opposite direction to the motion of the shot so that it always acts along the tangent to the trajectory. If u and v denote the horizontal and vertical components of the velocity of the shot at time t then the system can be represented by Fig. 2.2 where the resistance force D is given in magnitude by

$$D = 0.0045 \, (u^2 + v^2).$$

This can be resolved into its horizontal and vertical components, as shown, where $\tan \phi = v/u$.

Applying Newton's second law of motion horizontally and vertically gives

$$m \frac{du}{dt} = - \, 0.0045 \, (u^2 + v^2) \cos \phi,$$

$$m \frac{dv}{dt} = - \, mg - 0.0045 \, (u^2 + v^2) \sin \phi.$$

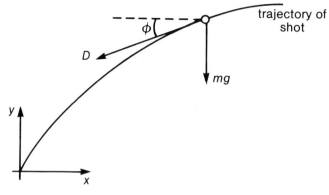

Fig. 2.2

Since the mass of a senior shot is 7.26 kg and

$$\sin \phi = \frac{v}{\sqrt{(u^2 + v^2)}}, \qquad \cos \phi = \frac{u}{\sqrt{(u^2 + v^2)}}$$

the equations of motion become

$$\frac{du}{dt} = - 0.00062 \, u \, \sqrt{(u^2 + v^2)},$$

$$\frac{dv}{dt} = - 9.81 - 0.00062 \, v \, \sqrt{(u^2 + v^2)} \; .$$

These are known as a pair of simultaneous differential equations and their solution is complicated by the fact that u and v occur in both.

Simple solution for u and v (and hence for x and y using integration) is not possible, although they can be solved using numerical techniques. Using the data given earlier ($\alpha = 40°$, $V = 13.7 \, \text{ms}^{-1}$, $h = 2.25 \, \text{m}$) gives a range of 20.9 m. As expected, the range is less when air resistance effects are taken into account. The difference is quite small, thus justifying the use of the much simpler result of equation (2.3) to determine the shot putter's range.

The throwing area
The rules for field events stipulate that the surface of the throwing area must be 'not more than 2.5 cm and not less than 1 cm below ground level'. It is therefore interesting to investigate the effect any violation of this rule has on the range of the throw, assuming V and α remain fixed at their earlier values. For example, suppose the surface of the throwing area is actually constructed at ground level then the small error in h is given by, at most

$$\delta h = 0.025 \, \text{m}.$$

If δR denotes the resulting small change in the range then, from the definition of a derivative

$$\frac{\delta R}{\delta h} \simeq \frac{dR}{dh}$$

so that differentiating equation (2.3) and simplifying the result gives

$$\delta R \simeq \frac{V \cos \alpha \cdot \delta h}{\sqrt{(V^2 \sin^2 \alpha + 2gh)}} . \tag{2.4}$$

Substituting the values used earlier together with $\delta h = 0.025$ m gives

$$\delta R = 0.024 \text{ m}.$$

This result shows the importance of constructing the throwing area correctly. A shot putter is not likely to be pleased to set a new record which is subsequently disallowed because of a little matter of δh!

2.2 HAMMER THROWING

The hammer used by athletes is very different from its domestic namesake. The athlete's hammer comprises a metal ball connected to a handle by a wire. The complete assembly weighs a minimum of 7.257 kg and is 1.175 m to 1.215 m in overall length.

The hammer thrower begins his action from the back of the throwing circle which is of radius 2.135 m. In order to be considered a successful throw the hammer must land within a marked sector of included angle 45° centred on the centre of the throwing cirle. Using a two-handed grip on the handle the athlete begins to rotate the hammer in a horizontal circle about his body. As the speed of rotation increases he begins to also rotate his body about an axis through the feet and inclined to the vertical and to move rapidly across the circle. Most hammer throwers complete three full turns during their passage across the circle although some of the more mobile athletes perform four revolutions. During this translation the plane in which the metal ball moves is inclined to the horizontal. Within this plane the path of the ball is such that it is near the ground while above the back of the throwing circle and high in the air towards the front of the throwing circle. As the athlete's feet approach the front of the circle the handle is released from the athlete's grip at which stage the complete device (ball, chain and handle) may be considered to be a projectile.

The formula developed in the previous section for the range of a shot put can also be used to determine the range of a hammer throw. Typical values of the release parameters V, α and h achieved by competent senior athletes are presented in the following table.

Parameter	Range of values
V	$20–26$ ms^{-1}
α	$40°–45°$
h	$1.4–2.2$ m

Using values of 24.0 ms^{-1}, $44°$ and 1.8 m respectively for V, α and h gives the range of the hammer throw as 60.49 m.

The hammer throw is a more difficult event to analyse than the shot put since the motion of the hammer is three-dimensional, at least before release. Considerable insight into the mechanics of the event can be obtained by simplifying the motion to a two-dimensional one. In this it is assumed that the athlete rotates about a fixed vertical axis and the plane in which the metal ball moves is horizontal. When a hammer thrower spins with a hammer, the athlete must apply a force (the centripetal force) to keep the hammer moving in a circular path, see Fig. 2.3. The athlete exerts this force by pulling on the hammer handle

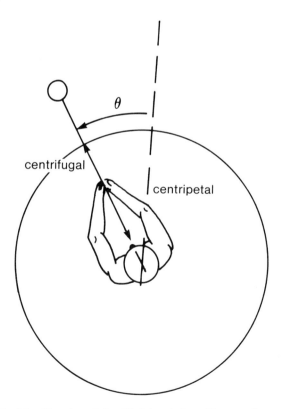

Fig. 2.3 – Plan view of simplified description of hammer thrower.

with a force towards the axis of rotation. The equal and opposite force that acts
on the athlete pulling him outward is called the centrifugal force. Together these
two forces are an illustration of Newton's third law of motion which states that
to every action there is an equal and opposite reaction.

If the radius of the circular path on which the metal ball, of mass m, moves
is denoted by l then the angular momentum of the hammer is

$$l \times ml \, \frac{d\theta}{dt} = ml^2 \, \frac{d\theta}{dt} \, ,$$

where θ denotes the angle through which the hammer has turned in time t. The
tangential equation of motion of the ball is

$$ml \, \frac{d^2\theta}{dt^2} = 0,$$

since there is no force acting on the ball in the tangential direction. Integration
of the equation of motion gives

$$\frac{d\theta}{dt} = \text{constant.}$$

Together with the expression for angular momentum it is seen that for the
hammer

angular momentum = constant.

The hammer throwing event is thus an illustration of the principle of conservation of angular momentum.

Since the range of any projectile throw is proportional to the square of the
release velocity, dramatic improvements in the range can be achieved by increasing the release velocity V. Although the angular momentum of the hammer has
previously been expressed in terms of angular quantities it can be expressed in
terms of rectilinear quantities as mlV, since $V = l \, (d\theta/dt)$. Consequently since the
angular momentum is conserved any increase in V must be accompanied by a
corresponding decrease in l, the radius of the metal ball's circular path. Hammer
throwers have a choice of two methods with which they can reduce l. They can
'sit back' into the throw during the last part of their final turn either by countering with the upper body, Fig. 2.4(a), or by countering with the hips, Fig. 2.4(b).
From Fig. 2.4 we see that countering with the upper body gives a smaller radius
of the circle of rotation of the hammer-head about the axis of rotation and thus
permits a higher velocity for the same angular momentum.

Reference to hammer throwing coaching manuals shows that the athletes
are encouraged to make their hands 'lead the hammer'. To understand the
meaning of this phrase consider Fig. 2.5. Fig. 2.5(a) illustrates the case in which
the line joining the ball to the hands passes through the axis of rotation while
Fig. 2.5(b) illustrates that in which the hands are ahead of, or 'lead', the ball.

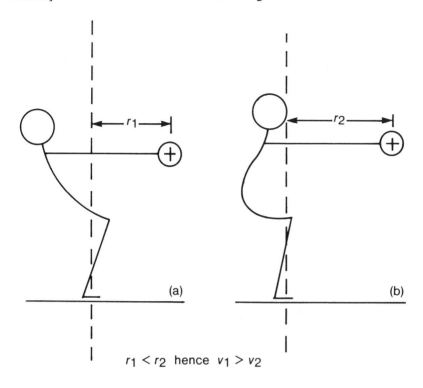

$r_1 < r_2$ hence $v_1 > v_2$

Fig. 2.4 – Countering with (a) the upper body, and (b) the hips.

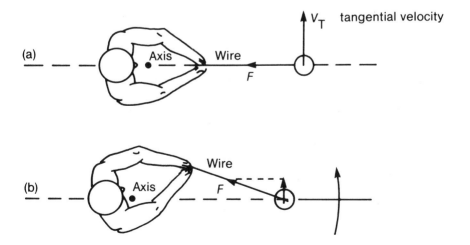

Fig. 2.5 – Diagram to illustrate benefit of hands 'leading' the hammer.

It can be seen in Fig. 2.5(b) that the force F exerted by the wire on the ball possesses a tangential component which acts in the direction of rotation. Associated with this a tangential acceleration which may be integrated to give a tangential velocity, additional to V_T of Fig. 2.5(a). Consequently there is some benefit to be had by causing the hands to 'lead' the hammer.

If you are familiar with vector, or cross, products there is no need to make the earlier simplifications that the athlete spins about a vertical axis and the hammer moves in a horizontal circle. The release velocity $\mathbf{v}$ of the hammer can be written as

$$\mathbf{v} = \mathbf{w}_\wedge \mathbf{r} \,,$$

where $\mathbf{w}$ represents the angular velocity vector of the hammer and athlete at the moment of release and $\mathbf{r}$ denotes the position vector of the hammer, also at the moment of release, relative to a set of fixed axes as shown in Fig. 2.6.

Suppose that the magnitude of the angular velocity at release is 14 radians per second then

$$\mathbf{w} = -14 \sin 42° \cos 80° \,\hat{\mathbf{i}} - 14 \sin 42° \sin 80° \,\hat{\mathbf{j}} + 14 \cos 42° \,\hat{\mathbf{k}}$$

$$= -1.627 \,\hat{\mathbf{i}} - 9.226 \,\hat{\mathbf{j}} + 10.404 \,\hat{\mathbf{k}}.$$

If the position vector of the hammer at the moment of release is

$$\mathbf{r} = 1.5 \,\hat{\mathbf{i}} - 1.03 \,\hat{\mathbf{j}} + 1.5 \,\hat{\mathbf{k}}$$

then the release velocity of the hammer is given by

$$\mathbf{v} = \mathbf{w}_\wedge \mathbf{r} = \begin{vmatrix} \hat{\mathbf{i}} & \hat{\mathbf{j}} & \hat{\mathbf{k}} \\ -1.627 & -9.226 & 10.404 \\ 1.5 & -1.03 & 1.5 \end{vmatrix}$$

$$= v_1 \hat{\mathbf{i}} + v_2 \hat{\mathbf{j}} + v_3 \hat{\mathbf{k}}$$

$$= -3.123 \,\hat{\mathbf{i}} + 18.046 \,\hat{\mathbf{j}} + 15.515 \,\hat{\mathbf{k}}.$$

The magnitude of the release velocity is therefore

$$|\mathbf{v}| = \sqrt{((-3.123)^2 + 18.046^2 + 15.515^2)} = 24 \text{ ms}^{-1},$$

and the direction of release of the hammer can be obtained from the velocity components as shown in Fig. 2.6 to give

$$\tan \alpha = \frac{v_3}{\sqrt{(v_1^2 + v_2^2)}}$$

$$= \frac{15.515}{\sqrt{((-3.123)^2 + 18.046^2)}} = 0.8472$$

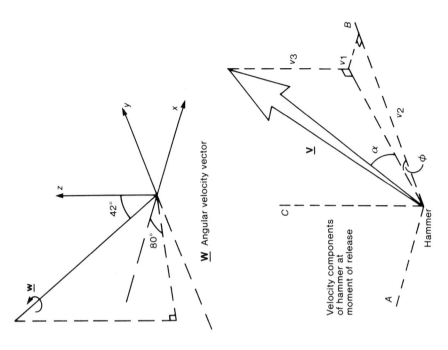

Fig. 2.6 – The hammer throw.

$$\alpha = 40.27°$$

$$\tan \phi = \left| \frac{v_1}{v_2} \right|$$

$$= \frac{3.123}{18.046} = 0.1731$$

$$\phi = 9.82°.$$

Immediately after release the hammer may be treated as a projectile released with a velocity of 24 ms^{-1} at an angle of $40.27°$ to the horizontal from a height of 1.5 m above the ground. Using the expression for the range of a projectile already developed in the section about the shot put, namely

$$R = \frac{V^2 \cos \alpha}{g} \left\{ \sin \alpha + \sqrt{\left(\sin^2 \alpha + \frac{2gh}{V^2} \right)} \right\}$$

the length of the hammer throw can be calculated as 59.64 m. In practice the length of a hammer throw is measured in the following way. The position at which the hammer lands is joined to the centre of the throwing circle by a straight line and the distance from the landing point to the intersection of the circle and the straight line is recorded.

2.3 THE OPTIMUM ANGLE OF RELEASE FOR SHOT AND HAMMER

The range R of a throw released with velocity V at an angle α to the horizontal from a height h above the ground has previously been shown to be given by

$$R = \frac{V^2 \cos \alpha}{g} \left\{ \sin \alpha + \sqrt{\left(\sin^2 \alpha + \frac{2gh}{V^2} \right)} \right\}. \tag{2.5}$$

Owing to the fact that the release velocity V occurs as a squared term it is clearly the most important of the parameters over which the throwing athlete has control, namely V, α and h.

Suppose we consider the shot put.

For a given release velocity V (say 13.7 ms^{-1}) and release height h (say 2.25 m) it is interesting to investigate how the range R varies with the release angle α. Table 2.1 contains the results for a wide range of values of α from $20°$ to $55°$.

Table 2.1
Variation of range R of a shot put with release angle α.

α (degrees)	20	25	30	35	40	45	50	55
R (m)	16.82	18.48	19.83	20.76	21.22	21.17	20.57	19.44

It is apparent from Table 2.1 that the optimum angle of release is somewhere in the range $35°$ to $45°$. It can be determined precisely by determining the derivative $dR/d\alpha$ and then solving the equation

$$\frac{dR}{d\alpha} = 0.$$

First rewrite equation (2.5) in the form

$$R = \frac{V^2}{2g} \sin 2\alpha + \frac{V^2}{g} \cdot \cos \alpha \cdot \left(\sin^2 \alpha + \frac{2gh}{V^2} \right)^{\frac{1}{2}}$$

and then differentiate with respect to α to give

$$\frac{dR}{d\alpha} = \frac{V^2}{g} \cos 2\alpha - \frac{V^2}{g} \sin \alpha \cdot \left(\sin^2 \alpha + \frac{2gh}{V^2} \right)^{\frac{1}{2}} + \frac{V^2}{g} \sin \alpha \cos^2 \alpha \left(\sin^2 \alpha + \frac{2gh}{V^2} \right)^{-\frac{1}{2}}.$$

To solve the equation $\dfrac{dR}{d\alpha} = 0$ we first obtain

$$\sin \alpha \left(\sin^2 \alpha + \frac{2gh}{V^2} \right)^{\frac{1}{2}} - \frac{\sin \alpha \cos^2 \alpha}{\left(\sin^2 \alpha + \frac{2gh}{V^2} \right)^{\frac{1}{2}}} = \cos 2\alpha$$

which can be rearranged to give

$$\sin \alpha \cdot \left(\frac{2gh}{V^2} - \cos 2\alpha \right) = \cos 2\alpha \left(\sin^2 \alpha + \frac{2gh}{V^2} \right)^{\frac{1}{2}}.$$

Squaring both sides of this equation and simplifying them gives

$$\frac{2gh}{V^2} \sin^2 \alpha - 2 \sin^2 \alpha \cdot \cos 2\alpha = \cos^2 2\alpha.$$

Next replace $\sin^2 \alpha$ in favour of $\cos 2\alpha$ as

$$\sin^2 \alpha = \frac{1}{2} (1 - \cos 2\alpha)$$

to give

$$\frac{gh}{V^2} (1 - \cos 2\alpha) - (1 - \cos 2\alpha) \cdot \cos 2\alpha = \cos^2 2\alpha$$

whence

$$\cos 2\alpha = \frac{gh}{(V^2 + gh)}$$

It is left as an exercise for the enthusiasts to establish that the value of α predicted by the above equation does indeed correspond to a maximum value for R!

For $V = 13.7$ ms^{-1} and $h = 2.25$ m the equation gives

$$\cos 2\alpha = \frac{9.81 \times 2.25}{(13.7^2 + 9.81 \times 2.25)}$$

$$= \frac{22.0725}{209.7625} = 0.10523$$

so $\alpha \simeq 42°$.

Thus to obtain the maximum range for a shot put which is released at 13.7 ms^{-1} at a height of 2.25 m above ground level, it should be released at an angle of approximately $42°$ to the horizontal.

It is left as an exercise for the reader to determine the optimum angle of release for a hammer thrown with a release velocity of 24 ms^{-1} from a height of 1.5 m.

Appendix III contains a BASIC computer program which you can use to investigate the effect on the optimum release angle of varying either V or α.

2.4 DISCUS AND JAVELIN

In the discus and javelin events aerodynamic forces play an important role. The effect of the air resistance is to reduce the horizontal component of velocity and hence the range. This adverse effect can be reduced by polishing the surface of the implement and of course by using aerodynamically efficient shapes.

The cross-section of the discus may be considered to be similar in shape to an aerofoil. Consequently as it travels through the air it experiences a lift force, just like an aeroplane wing, which causes the discus to remain in flight for longer than either a shot or a hammer.

The wind direction also has an effect. At athletics meetings one often sees the discus and javelin throwers carefully watching the flags around the arena. If possible they wait until they can throw into a headwind since this enhances the lift force and hence the time of flight. Intuitively one might expect them to favour the extra 'push' of a tailwind but in fact this has an adverse effect on the flight characteristics of the discus. Javelins too have an aerodynamic shape. Of interest is the way in which an athlete grips the javelin; the grip is such that on release the middle finger imparts a spin to the javelin about its longitudinal axis. This provides the javelin with the stability which is necessary for a smooth flight and a successful throw. Rifle bullets are caused to spin while in flight for exactly the same reason.

2.5 BASKETBALL SHOOTING

In basketball too, the release position of the ball is some height h above ground level. However, this time the purpose of the throw is to make the ball pass through the hoop instead of attempting to maximize the range of the throw. Nor is that all; it is important that the angle of entry of the ball into the hoop is correct since otherwise the ball will not pass through the hoop.

Angle of entry

If the basketball, of diameter 24.6 cm (the midpoint of the range of permitted diameters), approaches the hoop from directly above then it has a circular opening of diameter 45 cm through which it can pass. If the ball approaches from any other angle, say β to the horizontal (see Fig. 2.7), then the opening presented at right angles to the ball's path is an ellipse having one axis of length 45 cm and the other of length d cm where

$$d = 45 \sin \beta.$$

It is therefore evident that the ball will only pass through the ring provided that

$$45 \sin \beta > 24.6$$

so that

$$\beta > 33° \, 8'.$$

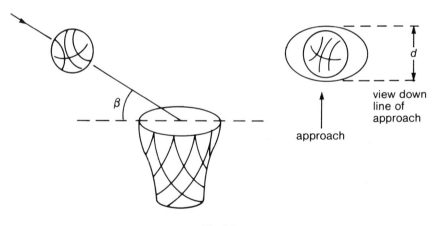

Fig. 2.7

Free shots

While it is possible to shoot the ball from any one of countless positions on a basketball court, the throw which is analysed here is the free shot. This is the shot awarded to a player who has been fouled and is taken from a fixed position.

To take the shot, the player stands behind the free throw line and attempts to throw the ball through the hoop. The point selected as the origin of coordinates is the centre of the ball at the moment of release, this point being approximately 2.15 m vertically above the free throw line (although the exact height will vary from player to player), see Fig. 2.8.

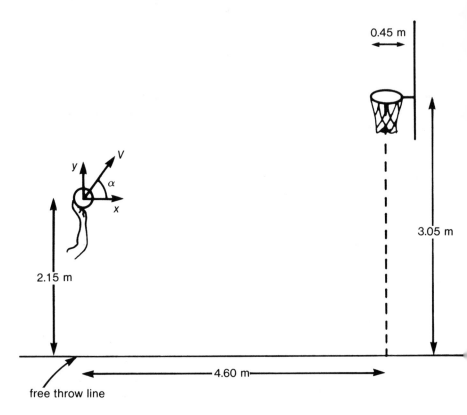

Fig. 2.8 – Basketball free throw dimensions.

If the coordinates of the centre of the hoop are (x_1, y_1) and the centre of the ball takes a time t to reach this point then using equations (2.1) and (2.2)

$$x_1 = (V \cos \alpha)t$$

and

$$y_1 = (V \sin \alpha)t - \frac{1}{2}gt^2,$$

where V and α denote the release velocity and release angle of projection respectively. Eliminating t between these two equations then gives

$$y_1 = x_1 \tan \alpha - \frac{gx_1^2}{2V^2} \sec^2\alpha. \tag{2.6}$$

A player may be awarded as many as three free shots and therefore in order to score from each he must be able to reproduce the same values of V and α in each shot. Of the two, it is easier to reproduce the value of V so that equation (2.6) may be solved to determine the required angle of release.

On replacing $\sec^2 \alpha$ in equation (2.6) using the trigonometric identity

$$\sec^2\alpha = 1 + \tan^2\alpha$$

the following quadratic equation in $\tan \alpha$ is obtained:

$$\frac{gx_1^2}{2V^2} \tan^2\alpha - x_1 \tan \alpha + y_1 + \frac{gx_1^2}{2V^2} = 0.$$

This can be solved to give

$$\tan \alpha = \frac{V^2}{gx_1} \left[1 \pm \sqrt{\left\{ 1 - \frac{2g}{V^2} \left(y_1 + \frac{gx_1^2}{2V^2} \right) \right\}} \right].$$

If the basketball centre is assumed to be released from a height of 2.15 m with a speed of 8 ms^{-1} then, using the values $g = 9.81$ ms^{-2}, $x_1 = 4.60$ m and $y_1 = 0.90$ m gives

$$\tan \alpha = 2.0939 \text{ or } 0.7426$$

so that

$$\alpha = 64° \ 28' \text{ or } 36° \ 36'.$$

In order to decide which angle to select, the ball's angle of entry to the hoop must now be considered (remember that it was shown that the angle of entry must not be less than $33° \ 8'$). From equations (2.1) and (2.2), the equation of the trajectory of the basketball is found by eliminating t to be

$$y = x \tan \alpha - \frac{gx^2}{2V^2} \sec^2\alpha$$

so that its slope at any point is given by

$$\frac{dy}{dx} = \tan \alpha - \frac{gx}{V^2} \sec^2\alpha.$$

At the basket, the slope of the trajectory is $-\tan \beta$ and thus

$$-\tan \beta = \tan \alpha - \frac{gx_1}{V^2} \sec^2\alpha.$$

Using the two values of α previously obtained then gives $\beta = 59° \, 34'$ (using $\alpha = 64° \, 28'$) and $\beta = 19° \, 21'$ (using $\alpha = 36° \, 36'$). Consequently, in order that a free shot released from the free throw line at a height of 2.15 m with a velocity of 8 ms^{-1} will score it must be released at an angle of $64° \, 28'$ to the horizontal, which explains the very acute angles of release seen in basketball games when a free throw is awarded.

Appendix IV contains a BASIC computer program which can be used to investigate the success, or failure, of a basketball free throw released with velocity V ms^{-1} from a height H m above the free throw line.

How high does the basketball reach?

Specialist basketball stadia are designed so that the ceiling is high enough not to interfere with the basketball trajectories normally encountered. The same cannot be said of all school and college gymnasia. It is quite likely that lights, climbing-rope frames etc. intrude into the space immediately below the ceiling and so reduce the effective ceiling height as far as basketball throws are concerned. Badminton is another sport which is adversely affected in this way.

It is thus sensible to investigate the height to which a basketball free throw will rise. Obviously it will depend on the values of the release height, release angle and release velocity of the basketball but we can obtain an idea of the order of magnitude of the height reached if we use the values of the basketball release parameters introduced earlier, namely

$$h = 2.15 \text{ m}, V = 8 \text{ ms}^{-1}, \alpha = 64° \, 28'.$$

The basketball will stop rising when its vertical component of velocity becomes zero. At time t s the vertical displacement y m of the basketball has previously been shown to be

$$y = (V \sin \alpha)t - \frac{1}{2} gt^2.$$

The vertical component of velocity v ms^{-1} can be obtained from this by differentiating with respect to t to give

$$v = V \sin \alpha - gt.$$

The basketball thus stops rising vertically at time T s where

$$T = \frac{V \sin \alpha}{g}$$

at which time the vertical displacement is

$$y = (V \sin \alpha) \left(\frac{V \sin \alpha}{g} \right) - \frac{1}{2} g \left(\frac{V \sin \alpha}{g} \right)^2 = \frac{V^2 \sin^2 \alpha}{2g}.$$

The height reached by the basketball centre above ground level is thus

$$h + \frac{V^2 \sin^2 \alpha}{2g} \; .$$

Substituting the values of V, α and h stated earlier then gives the height reached as

$$2.15 + \frac{(8 \sin 64° \; 28')^2}{2 \times 9.81} = 4.81 \text{ m}$$

It is thus not surprising that one sometimes experiences problems in school gymnasia due to badly positioned light fittings etc.

You may like to carry out a similar calculation for the shot putting event to see whether indoor throwing would be a practical proposition (it could solve the weather problem associated with winter training) always of course assuming that the floor could stand the strain!

3

Jumping

3.1 THE STRADDLE AND FOSBURY FLOP HIGH JUMP TECHNIQUES

The two most frequently seen high jump techniques are the straddle and the Fosbury flop. Figure 3.1 shows the body position for each technique at the instant of crossing the bar.

Earlier in the history of the event, the most popular technique was the scissors jump, see Fig. 3.1. This had the advantage that the athlete landed feet first — essential in those early days when the landing areas were often just grass! Although simple to master, the scissors technique was mechanically very inefficient since the centre of mass of the jumper had to be raised a considerable height above the bar.

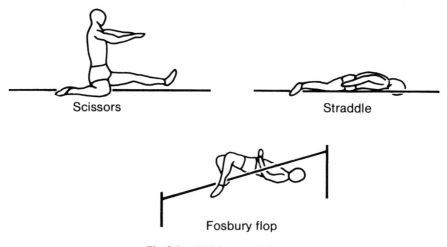

Fig. 3.1 — High jump techniques.

In the 1930s as both training methods and landing areas improved two new jumping techniques evolved (the Eastern cut-off and the Western roll) and from these was developed the straddle jump. In this the athlete 'wraps' himself around the bar. This technique is mechanically much more efficient since the centre of mass need now only be raised to just above the level of the bar.

No major changes in high jump technique then occurred until 1968 when Richard Fosbury (USA) revolutionized high jump ideas with his 'flop' technique, in which the athlete travels backwards over the bar with his back arched. Compared with other techniques the Fosbury flop demands exceptional mobility on the part of the athlete. It is perhaps not altogether surprising that the flop should have burst upon the athletics world in the late nineteen-sixties, a time when gymnastics (which also demands mobility) was gaining popularity.

An analysis of the Fosbury flop shows that it is possible for the high jumper to clear the bar while his centre of gravity passes beneath the bar. The implication of this is that a jumper using the Fosbury technique should be able to clear a given height with less thrust off the ground than if he was using some other technique. Hence for a given thrust the Fosbury flopper should theoretically be able to jump higher.

Whichever technique is employed, the fundamental problem faced by the high jumper is to convert the horizontal approach run into vertical lift in order to execute the jump.

Suppose the athlete is of mass m and that he approaches the bar with a horizontal velocity U. At take-off, assume he experiences a vertical impulse I at the ground and that immediately after take-off the horizontal and vertical velocity components of his centre of gravity are u and v respectively. Application of the principle of conservation of momentum in both the horizontal and vertical directions results in

$$m(u - U) = 0 \qquad (3.1)$$

and

$$m(v - 0) = I, \qquad (3.2)$$

whence

$$u = U \text{ and } v = I/m. \qquad (3.3)$$

If the centre of mass of the jumper is at height h above the ground at the moment of take-off then on take-off the jumper becomes a projectile with velocity components as shown in Fig. 3.2. Applying Newton's second law of motion both horizontally and vertically gives

$$m \frac{d^2 x}{d t^2} = 0 \qquad (3.4)$$

and

$$m \frac{d^2 y}{d t^2} = -mg , \qquad (3.5)$$

if air resistance effects are ignored.

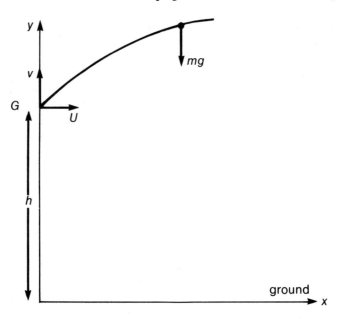

Fig. 3.2 – Release parameters of trajectory of centre of mass of a high-jumper.

Integrating these two differential equations then gives

$$x = Ut \tag{3.6}$$

and

$$y = -\frac{1}{2} gt^2 + vt + h. \tag{3.7}$$

The quantity of interest is the maximum value attained by y, which will occur at the instant when $dy/dt = 0$.

From equation (3.7),

$$\frac{dy}{dt} = -gt + v,$$

so y attains its maximum value when $t = v/g$. This maximum value is found from equation (3.7) to be

$$y_{max} = \frac{v^2}{2g} + h, \tag{3.8}$$

where h represents the vertical displacement of the athlete's centre of gravity at the moment of take-off.

The value of h will depend upon the position of the jumper's body at the moment of take-off. Before h can be calculated, a mechanical model of the athlete must be obtained.

While it is appreciated that an athlete is a very complicated biomechanical system, a realistic yet simple model comprising nine hinged rods plus a disc for the head is proposed.

Figure 3.3(a) shows this model with the lengths and masses of the various elements given as fractions of the athlete's overall height (l) and mass (m).

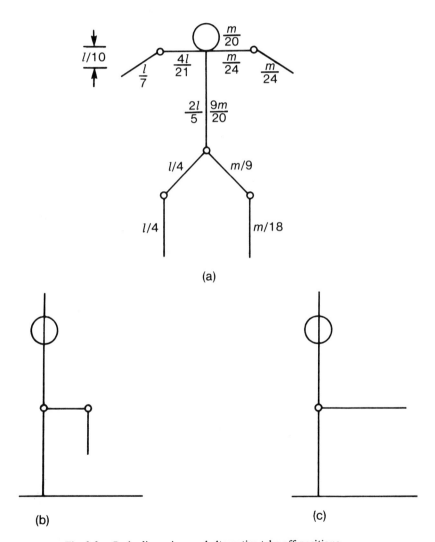

(a)

(b)   (c)

Fig. 3.3 — Body dimensions and alternative take-off positions.

Figure 3.3(b) represents the jumper at the instant of take-off with both arms raised above the head and the free leg bent. (There are alternative body positions on take-off, for example using a straight free leg, see Fig. 3.3(c), and any coaching manual on the high jump will discuss the relative merits of these.) With the high jumper in the take-off position shown in Fig. 3.4 the height (h) of the centre of mass above ground level can be found by referring to the figure and taking moments about the ground to give

$$mh = \frac{m}{18} \cdot \frac{l}{8} + \frac{m}{9} \cdot \frac{3l}{8} + \frac{m}{18} \cdot \frac{3l}{8} + \frac{m}{9} \cdot \frac{l}{2} + \frac{9m}{20} \cdot \frac{7l}{10}$$

$$+ \frac{m}{12} \cdot \frac{209l}{210} + \frac{m}{20} \cdot \frac{19l}{20} + \frac{m}{12} \cdot \frac{244l}{210}$$

$$= ml \left(\frac{1}{144} + \frac{1}{24} + \frac{1}{48} + \frac{1}{18} + \frac{63}{200} + \frac{209}{2520} + \frac{19}{400} + \frac{61}{630} \right)$$

so

$$h = 0.667l.$$

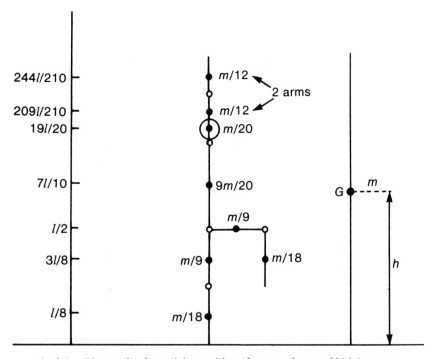

Fig. 3.4 – Diagram for determining position of centre of mass of high jumper at the instant of take-off.

Thus for the case of a jumper who is 1.98 m tall, $h = 1.32$ m while for a 1.83 m tall jumper $h = 1.22$ m. Hence the taller athlete has a distinct advantage (remember $y_{max} = v^2/2g + h$). It is thus most important that a high jumper should choose his parents carefully! The interested reader may care to determine h for the alternative 'straight leg' take-off position shown in Fig. 3.3(c) ($h = 0.674l$). Although this 'straight leg' technique gives a larger value for h it is physically very demanding and only the strongest athletes use it.

The next question to answer is 'how high does the jumper need to raise his centre of mass to clear a particular height of bar?' To answer this, it is necessary to examine each jumping technique separately.

In the straddle jump, the athlete's body is horizontal and parallel to the bar as the bar is cleared. As the athlete reaches the limits of his jumping ability, the clearance between his body and the bar will be minimal and so it is assumed that the height to which the athlete's centre of mass is raised is equal to the bar height. From equations (3.3) and (3.8) the take-off impulse I may be obtained as

$$I^2 = 2m^2g(y_{max} - h) \tag{3.9}$$

Thus for a 1.98 m tall high jumper (for whom $h = 1.32$ m) clearing a 2.13 m jump using the straddle technique

$$I_s^2 = 2m^2g(2.13 - 1.32)$$

$$= 2m^2g \times 0.81$$

The next section investigates the position of the centre of mass of a 1.98 m tall 'Fosbury flopper' clearing the same 2.13 m jump. Photographic evidence suggests that as the jumper clears the bar, his body is, typically, in the position shown in Fig. 3.5.

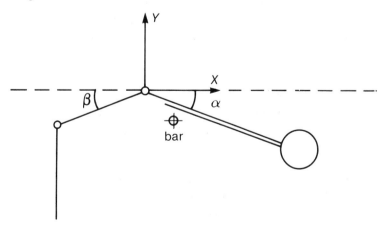

Fig. 3.5 – Typical position adopted in clearance of the bar using the Fosbury flop technique.

Relative to a set of axes located at the hips the coordinates of the centre of mass are given by

$$(\overline{X}, \overline{Y}) = (\frac{251}{1680} l \cos \alpha - \frac{1}{18} l \cos \beta, - \frac{251}{1680} l \sin \alpha - \frac{1}{18} l \sin \beta - \frac{1}{72} l)$$

A typical value for both α and β is $20°$ so that, with $l = 1.98$ m,

$$(\overline{X}, \overline{Y}) = (0.175, -0.166).$$

This means that at the highest point of its trajectory the mass centre is 0.166 m below the hips. This high point should be on a vertical line drawn through the bar at this instant. For the above values of $(\overline{X}, \overline{Y})$ this will occur when the hip joint is 0.06 m above the bar, i.e. the centre of mass is 0.10 m *below* the bar.

The Fosbury flopper therefore need only raise his centre of mass to a height of $y_{max} = 2.03$ m in order to clear the bar (set at 2.13 m). Thus from equation (3.9), for the Fosbury flop

$$I_F^2 = 2m^2g (2.03 - 1.32)$$

$$= 2m^2g \times 0.71.$$

The ratio of these impulses for the two different jumping techniques is thus given by

$$\frac{I_F}{I_S} = 0.936.$$

The above result means that for a 2.13 m jump, a jumper using the Fosbury flop technique need only exert about 94% of the thrust required using the straddle technique. Put another way, for a given impulse the 'flopper' can jump higher than the 'straddler'. Obviously there is more to high jumping than just raising the centre of mass to a given height, but coaches agree that this is the most important factor.

3.2 THE POLE VAULT

In this event the athlete carries a long flexible pole, held close to one end with a two-handed grip and sprints down a track some forty to forty-five metres in length towards a horizontal cross-bar over which he must vault with the aid of the flexible pole.

As he nears the vertical plane containing the cross-bar, he lowers the free end of the pole into a box set in the ground at the end of the run-up track. Since the pole is flexible this sudden anchoring of one end causes it to bend and compress thus causing potential energy to be stored in the pole, in the same way that potential energy can be stored in a spring by compressing it. This is not the only energy source in the system: the pole vaulter himself possesses considerable kinetic energy, due to his run-up.

The principle of conservation of energy states that energy can be neither created nor destroyed, but only converted into different forms. Thus the total energy possessed by the vaulter and pole at take-off is converted into potential energy and kinetic energy of rotation which enables the vaulter to raise himself and the pole up to the vertical and, for the vaulter, beyond and over the bar.

Up until about twenty-five years ago the pole used at major meetings was rigid, made of bamboo wood and, later, metal. To-day the athletes use flexible poles made of glass fibre which are constructed to withstand the stresses incurred when the pole is bent through a right angle over its length (i.e. at take-off the bottom end of the pole is vertical and the top end is horizontal). With rigid poles the distance from the end which is 'planted' in the box to the hands was less than with modern flexible poles. This is because the pendulum arc of the vaulter swinging with a rigid pole had to be of smaller radius since otherwise the energy of the system was insufficient to raise the vaulter to the vertical! Owing to the flexible pole's greater ability to store energy the hand grip can be higher up the pole.

As the vaulter approaches the box carrying a flexible pole, the pole and vaulter system possesses kinetic energy of amount

$$\frac{1}{2} (m_A + m_p) V^2 ,$$

where V denotes the vaulter's velocity at take-off, m_A denotes his mass and m_p denotes the mass of the pole.

After the pole has been 'planted' in the box one end may be considered fixed and the flexible pole begins to deform until ultimately the pole has assumed a shape with the free end horizontal. Momentarily it stops in this position before the free end A begins to both recoil and rotate about the box. Assuming that immediately after the plant the vaulter continues horizontally with approximately the same velocity as he had immediately prior to the plant then the original kinetic energy of the pole is converted in potential energy possessed by the pole due to its deformation. This potential energy is subsequently returned to the system — part is used to raise the pole to the vertical and the remainder is available to assist in raising the vaulter's centre of mass. Since the mass of the pole is very much less than that of the vaulter the potential energy stored in the pole, which is equal to the kinetic energy it acquired in the run-up, is much less than the kinetic energy of the vaulter and may be ignored in a simple analysis.

If it is assumed that after take-off the energy exchange is one hundred per cent efficient (which it is not — losses occur due to the impact of the pole with the box, the backward thrust of the ground on the take-off foot and the bending of the pole) then the principle of conservation of energy may be expressed as

Total energy at take-off = Total energy when pole vaulter is at the top of his trajectory

i.e. $\dfrac{1}{2} mV^2 = mgh$

so
$$h = \frac{V^2}{2g},$$

where m denotes the mass of the vaulter and pole, g the acceleration due to gravity, h the rise of the vaulter's centre of mass above its horizontal level at take-off and V is the vaulter's velocity at the end of his run-up. Strictly speaking h is the rise of the centre of mass of the combined vaulter *and* pole although since the pole is so much lighter than the athlete, this centre of mass will be virtually the same as that of the vaulter alone. A fair approximation to V is given by the vaulter's average velocity for a 100 m sprint (this is much more easily obtained than an instantaneous velocity at some intermediate distance of 40 m or 45 m). Ideally the vaulter should be timed while carrying his pole. For an athlete who can run the 100 m in 11 s the average velocity is 9.09 ms^{-1}. Using the expression just obtained for h, the height through which his centre of mass is raised above its initial level is 4.21 m. In order to determine the theoretical height cleared by the vaulter we must add the height above ground level of his centre of mass at the moment of take-off. A typical value for this is approximately 1 m although obviously it will vary both with the physique of the vaulter and the exact body configuration at take-off.

For the fictitious vaulter we have introduced, the elementary application of the principle of conservation of energy gives a pole vault performance of 5.21 m. For comparison purposes the world record at the time of writing is 5.75 m, held jointly by Volz (USA) and Bellot (France).

Athletics coaching manuals divide the pole vault into six sections. Beginning with (i) the run-up these are (ii) the plant, (iii) the take-off, (iv) the swing and rock back, (v) the pull up, and (vi) the clearance. Each of these phases is interesting from a mechanics point of view.

(i) The run-up and (ii) the plant (Fig. 3.6(a))

The run-up is the first phase of the event and is generally considered by the coaches to be most important. The vaulter's objective is to achieve his maximum controlled speed during the last few strides in order that, at take-off, he has maximum horizontal velocity. The emphasis is on the word 'controlled' since the vaulter is not only sprinting but carrying a long pole which he holds close to one end. Later in this section we shall examine the pole carrying more closely. Unless the approach is controlled and relaxed the vaulter's main concern is likely to be stability and not sprinting speed! The length of the approach run will obviously vary with the individual but is generally about forty metres.

As the jumping area is neared, the end of the pole remote from the hands is lowered (planted) into the box which is situated immediately in front of the vertical plane containing the cross-bar which the vaulter must clear. This phase is called the plant; the effect is to anchor one end of the pole while the other end, held by the vaulter, is still travelling horizontally at high speed. The net result is to bend and compress the pole thereby storing some energy in the pole, which is retrieved later as potential energy available for raising the vaulter. The sudden anchoring also introduces an angular motion, about the box, enabling both the pole and the vaulter to rotate towards the vertical.

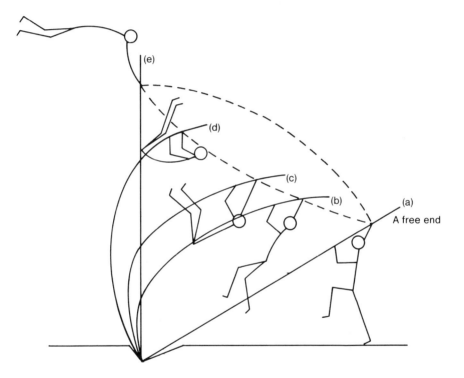

Fig. 3.6 – Sequence of pole and body positions adopted by pole-vaulter.

(iii) The take-off (Fig. 3.6(b))

In order to keep the pole moving forward at take-off the force exerted by the hands on the pole must be directed ahead of the box so that its moment about the box is in the correct (anticlockwise) sense (see Fig. 3.7(b)). This is accomplished by bending the lower arm which causes the vaulter's centre of mass to move forwards and closer to the pole. This reduces the adverse clockwise moment

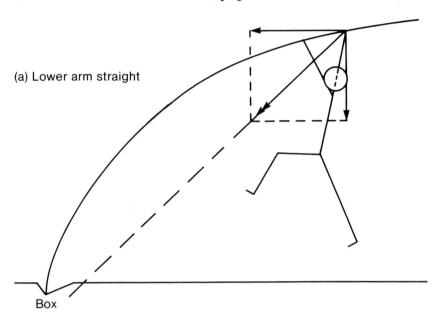

(a) Lower arm straight

Box

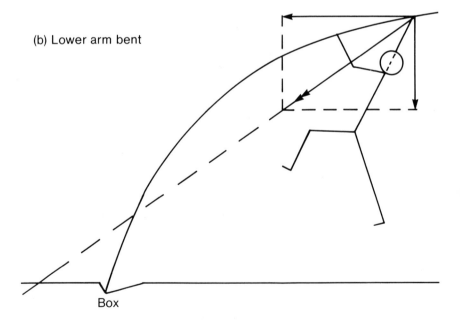

(b) Lower arm bent

Box

Fig. 3.7 — Diagram to illustrate how bending of the lower arm aids in directing the take-off force ahead of the box.

of the vaulter's weight about the pivot (the box), which tends to pull the free end of the pole down towards the ground, and also facilitates the subsequent swing of the legs and hips. At take-off the vertical component of the force should be little more than the vaulter's body weight. Any increase in the vertical component at the expense of the horizontal component could direct the result-ant force behind the box (see Fig. 3.7(a)). The penetration of the pole is aided at take-off if the vaulter (assumed to be right-handed) momentarily extends his right leg downwards from its current flexed at the knee configuration. This moves his centre of mass closer to the pivot (the box) than it would otherwise be and consequently, just like a metronome, increases the angular speed of the pole and vaulter in accordance with the principle of conservation of angular momentum. Remember angular momentum $= mr^2 w$, so any reduction in r must be accompanied by an increase in angular velocity w. Since angular momen-tum can also be expressed in terms of rectilinear quantities as mrv where v is the velocity of the centre of mass then it can be seen that dropping the right leg also has the effect of maintaining the forward velocity v of the vaulter with consequent advantage to the forward and upward motion of the pole (see Fig. 3.8).

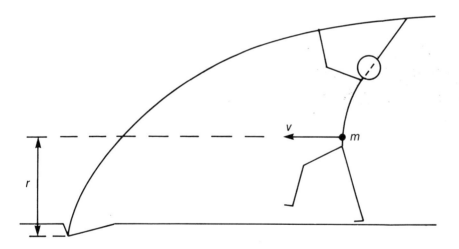

Fig. 3.8 – A reduction in r leads to an increase in v since the angular momentum (mrv) is conserved.

(iv) The swing and rock back (Fig. 3.6(c) and (d))
During this phase, the bend in the pole increases to a maximum in which both the free end of the pole (adjacent to the hands) and the vaulter's back are parallel to the ground. Up to this time the athlete's arms and shoulders remain rigid so

that his body stays behind the pole and the pole continues to be driven forwards and upwards. Towards the end of this phase, the legs and hips are flexed rapidly and rotated backwards, over the head, about the shoulders.

(v) The pull up and (vi) the clearance (Fig. 3.6(e))

Once the hips have rotated upwards until they are against the pole, the lower arm is brought closer to the pole thereby reducing the radius of rotation. At the same time the vaulter will feel the pole begin to recoil and lift him as it straightens; this is the release of the potential energy stored in the pole when it was originally bent. When the pole is almost straight and vertical the vaulter vigorously pulls his body upwards by both arms. He is now in a feet uppermost position with his legs and body parallel to the pole. From this position the impulse of the recoil of the pole and the arm pull enables him to 'fly' off the upper end of the pole, arch his body and with his back uppermost clear the cross-bar.

The carrying of the pole is itself interesting to analyse. During the run-up the pole is carried close to the vaulter's right hip (assuming a right-handed vaulter) with the thumb of the lower (left) hand under the pole to support the weight and the thumb of the upper (right) hand pressing down in order to hold the tip of the pole up (see Fig. 3.9). The coaching manuals measure 'lower' and 'upper' relative to the planted end of the pole. There are three ways to carry the pole: they are

(1) the high carry, with the free end well above the head height. This enables the vaulter to extend the right arm more and so move easily to apply sufficient downward force with the right hand but at the expense of a large frontal area which can cause aerodynamic troubles on a windy day;

(2) the medium carry, in which the free end is at about head height;

(3) the parallel carry, in which the pole is held parallel to the ground.

While (2) and (3) overcome the problem of the large frontal area of the pole they make it more dificult to apply the necessary downward force with the right-hand since the arm is not so extended.

The poles used in current top-class competition are 4.27 m, 4.57 m or 4.87 m in length. The distance from the end which is eventually 'planted' in the box to the hand hold position varies with the length of the pole but for a 4.57 m pole the hand grip will typically be between 4.10 m and 4.25 m from the end with the hands placed a distance apart of some 0.43 m.

In order to assess the forces applied by the hands we shall assume a parallel carry of a 4.57 m pole with the hands 0.43 m apart and centred at a distance 4.17 m (the midpoint of the range 4.10 m to 4.25 m) from one end (see Fig. 3.9).

P: Thumb beneath pole and fingers above
Q: Thumb above pole and fingers below

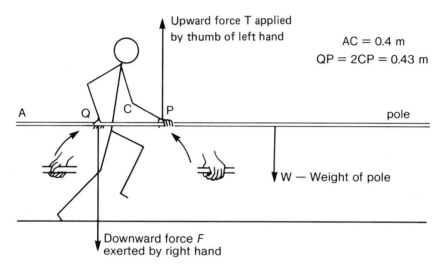

Fig. 3.9 – The carry.

Taking moments about about the fulcrum P then gives

$$W \times \left(\frac{4.57}{2} - 0.615 \right) = F \times 0.43$$

$$F = \frac{W \times 1.67}{0.43}$$

$$F \simeq 3.9\,W,$$

and resolving the forces vertically gives

$$T = F + W$$

i.e.

$$T = 4.9\,W.$$

To the vaulter the pole therefore appears to be approximately four to five times its actual weight while being carried and so represents a significant extra burden during the run-up phase.

Finally, it is interesting to speculate about how much higher pole-vaulters might be expected to reach using their present equipment and techniques.

Simple energy considerations suggest that it should be possible to reach approximately 7 m. The kinetic energy of an athlete running at 9.09 ms^{-1} (11s for the 100 m) is sufficient to raise his centre of mass 4.21 m beyond its initial height above ground level of approximately 1 m. Pole-vaulters are competent gymnasts and it is therefore reasonable to expect them to be able to pull themselves up and perform a hand stand on the pole, as if their hand—hold position on the pole was fixed in space. This would raise the centre of mass through approximately 2.1 m giving a total of some 7.3 m. With allowance made for an efficiency of less than one hundred per cent it should be possible to increase the world record to about 7 m. Forthcoming years will determine the degree to which this is approached.

3.3 THE LONG JUMP

Introduction

A quantitative analysis of the long jump (neglecting the air resistance experienced by the athlete) requires a knowledge of the equations of motion of a body moving under a constant acceleration (gravity) and the principle of conservation of momentum. Since it is very difficult to measure the angular momentum of an athlete whose position is constantly changing, the principle of conservation of angular momentum is only used qualitatively in the following analysis of long jumping techniques.

The most casual observation of long jumping reveals several features:

(a) at take-off, the athlete's centre of mass is above its level on landing;
(b) while in the air, the athlete usually uses his legs in an action similar to cycling;
(c) the arms are used to complement the leg action.

It is possible to use observation (a) to obtain an expression for the length of the jump in terms of various parameters which can be easily measured.

Determination of the length of the jump

Figure 3.10 shows the typical body position adopted by a long jumper at take-off and landing. At take-off the athlete's centre of mass is located a horizontal distance T ahead of the take-off board and on landing it is a distance L behind the athlete's heels. The length of the jump is actually measured from the take-off board to the imprint, nearest to the take-off board, made in the sand by the athlete. In normal circumstances this will be the landing position of the athlete's heels. Thus,

$$\text{length of jump} = T + R + L \, ,$$

where R denotes the range of the trajectory of the athlete's centre of mass.

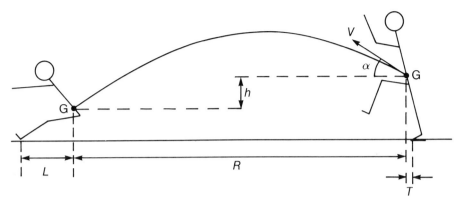

Fig. 3.10 – Values of T and L are in the ranges $0.3 - 0.4$ m and $0.75 - 1.0$ m respectively. Recorded value of the long jump $= T + R + L$.

It has been established elsewhere in the text that

$$R = \frac{V^2\cos\alpha}{g}\left\{\sin\alpha + \sqrt{\left(\sin^2\alpha + \frac{2gh}{V^2}\right)}\right\},$$

where V = take-off velocity of the athlete, and α = take-off angle of the athlete measured from the horizontal, and this time h = difference in heights above ground level of the athlete's centre of mass at take-off and landing.

Since the range R is proportional to the square of the take-off velocity then it will be most affected by changes which the athlete can produce in V compared with the effect of changes in α and h. This explains why coaches concentrate so strongly on developing an athlete's run-up and consequent take-off velocity.

Appendix II contains a BASIC program which you can use to determine the length of a long jump for values of V, α, h, L and T which you input. The program contains typical ranges of values for these quantities, they are reproduced below for your convenience. The values were obtained from measurement of still photographs taken from a high-speed film of the long jump event.

Parameter	Typical range of values
V	$8–10$ ms^{-1}
α	$18°–22°$
h	$0.4–0.6$ m
L	$0.75–1.0$ m
T	$0.3–0.4$ m

For example, suppose that

$$V = 9 \text{ ms}^{-1} \quad \alpha = 20° \quad \text{and} \quad h = 0.5 \text{ m}$$

then

$$R = 6.44 \text{ m}.$$

With the addition of allowances for L and T, say 0.8 m and 0.35 m respectively the length of the jump is

$$0.35 + 6.44 + 0.8 = 7.59 \text{ m}.$$

The world record for the long jump is currently 8.90 m, set by R. Beamon (USA) in 1968 at Mexico City. This is generally regarded as an exceptional jump and it has hardly been approached since. The projectile analysis presented here can thus be considered to give a reasonable model of long jumping. Two obvious refinements would be to include the effects of air resistance and the inertia of the various body segments (as opposed to treating the athlete as a particle). The resulting model would then be considerably more complex.

The three phases of the jump
Observations (b) and (c) can be explained using a qualitative analysis of the event. For this analysis, the event is divided into three phases, (a) approach, (b) take-off and (c) flight and landing.

Approach and take-off
The jumper is concerned with taking off from as close to the front of the marker board as possible and converting horizontal speed into vertical lift. It is this lift which is of paramount concern to the jumper in his last few strides.

It is no coincidence that top-class long jumpers also have good performances in the 100 m sprint. However, the 100 m times do not correlate exactly with long jump results since it is the speed attained over approximately the first 40 m of a sprint which is important to the long jumper. The length of the approach run will vary with the athlete but must be long enough to enable the athlete to reach the take-off board at top speed and in the best position to accurately plant the take-off foot on the take-off board.

During the last few strides of the run-up, the long jumper prepares for the take-off. The athlete adopts a more upright position since the forward lean adopted by sprinters would prevent good lift at take-off. The penultimate stride is usually slightly lengthened since this produces a lowering of the hips and thus of the body's centre of gravity so giving a longer path for acceleration of the centre of gravity.

The take-off foot will land slightly in front of the vertical projection of the body's centre of mass which then rotates about the foot, as a fulcrum, so that as the take-off foot leaves the board force is applied below and behind the centre of mass. If the take-off foot is too far ahead of the body it will have a braking effect while if it is too close to the body insufficient drive results. As the body weight passes over the take-off foot the jumping leg extends vigorously to drive the athlete upwards.

The free leg (the one not used for take-off) also drives vigorously upwards in a well flexed position at the knee. The reason for being flexed at the knee is that in its rotation about the hips the moment of inertia of the free leg will be lower than if the leg is straight. Consequently the angular momentum will be greater, thus enabling the free leg drive to be accomplished quickly. This vigorous drive of the free leg produces an equal and opposite downward reaction (Newton's third law of motion) on the take-off leg which increases the propulsive force at take-off. Finally, the propulsive force is further enhanced by driving strongly upwards with the arm on the side opposite to the free leg.

Flight and landing
Once the athlete has left the take-off board, the path followed by the mass centre cannot be influenced by any action of the athlete. Ignoring air resistance, both the linear and the angular momentum possessed by the athlete at take-off are conserved. Nevertheless, one sees considerable movements of the athlete's limbs during the flight phase of the jump. The reasons for this are twofold, first the limbs are moved to obtain a more favourable landing position and secondly they are moved to counteract the forward rotation set up by the leg thrust being developed from behind the athlete's centre of mass at take-off.

The aim is to delay the trunk's forward speed and allow the legs time and space to come through into a good landing position. This rotation can be controlled by attaining a long thin shape and avoiding small shapes while in the air. This means that the athlete's moment of inertia about the axis of rotation is large and consequently via the principle of conservation of angular momentum, the angular speed of rotation is reduced.

Jumping styles
With the athlete clear of the ground, we may now examine the styles in the air which bring about the flight objectives described above. Several styles are in use. The most elementary is the 'sail'; the major current ones being the 'hang' and the '1½ (or 2½) hitch kick'.

(i)   The 'sail':
      Although this technique is most inefficient and is not now used at all by good-class jumpers, it is worthy of a few comments since it is the 'natural' long jumping style adopted by children.

      When using this technique, the child will run to the board, take off then immediately adopt the legs forward position for landing. No attempt is made to counteract the forward rotation introduced at take-off. This causes the heels to drop prematurely, with a consequent shortening of the jump.

(ii)   The 'hang':
        After take-off the flexed free leg straightens and drops to join the jumping
        leg. The lower parts of both legs are close together at a right angle with the
        thighs. The vigour of this pull back straightens up the trunk and the athlete
        travels half the jumping distance in this position with the chest elevated
        and the eyes looking straight ahead. The arms are held back ready to come
        through on landing. For landing, the legs are brought through bent, and
        straightened later. If the legs are straightened prematurely the body will
        be dragged down in reaction. Landing efficiency is increased if immediately
        before landing the arms are thrown forwards from behind the jumper's
        body. This assists the forward pivoting of the body and minimises the risk
        of falling back into the sand. Occasionally one sees an athlete 'fall out
        sideways' after landing. This is done because there is not sufficient angular
        momentum to pivot forward over the feet and the athlete would otherwise
        fall back in the sand. Since the length of jump is determined by the
        rearmost mark made by the athlete in the sand, falling backwards must be
        avoided at all costs!

(iii)   The 'hitch kick':
        In this technique the athlete appears to attempt to run in the air. After
        take-off the free leg is straightened and moved backwards, while at the
        same time the jumping leg (now bent) is brought rapidly forward. Thus the
        angular momentum of the straight leg is balanced by the angular momentum
        of the bent leg. From here the bent take-off leg straightens out in pre-
        paration for the landing. The straightened leg completes its backwards
        swing, folds up and is then brought forward to join the other leg, already
        extended, preparatory to landing. If a long jumper is jumping particularly
        far, it is possible that the 1½ strides will be completed well before the heels
        strike the sand, causing the heels to drop due to forward rotation. This can
        be countered by employing an extra stride while in the air to give the 2½
        hitch kick.

3.4 THE LONG JUMP WORLD RECORD – AN ANALYSIS

The current world record of 8.90 m was established by Bob Beamon, of the
United States of America, at the 1968 Olympic Games in Mexico City when he
increased the previous world record by an astounding 0.55 m. Beamon's record
has rarely been approached since and there have been suggestions the result was,
at least in part, due to the rarefied air in Mexico City (2600 m above sea level).
The rarefied air would have the effect of reducing the drag force experienced by
the long jumper.
        This explanation would seem to be of little substance since the high jump,
shot and other events which also involve the motion of a body through the air

in the presence of a resistance force did not have similarly outstanding world records established in Mexico. It would therefore appear that Beamon's jump was a superlative performance, the fact that the event took place at altitude being of very little consequence.

If we treat the long jumper as a particle moving under the effects of gravity and air resistance we can show that the difference in values of the air density between sea level and Mexico City leads to an increase in the length of the jump, over its sea level value, of approximately 0.04 m. Thus Beamon's jump was, quite simply, exceptional.

Figure 2.2 may be considered to represent a long jumper as a particle of mass m at some time t after take-off. $\mathbf{D}$ represents the air resistance force. Applying Newton's second law of motion to the particle gives

$$m\mathbf{a} = m\mathbf{g} + \mathbf{D}$$

where $\mathbf{a}$ denotes the acceleration of the particle.

In order to make any further progress in this analysis, the mathematical nature of the aerodynamic drag force must be ascertained. This force has been found experimentally to be proportional to

(i)   the air density, ρ,
(ii)   the square of the body's velocity, V^2, and
(iii)   the cross-sectional area A which the body presents to the air

i.e. $D \propto \rho V^2 A$.

Introducing C_D, a constant known as the drag coefficient, the magnitude of the drag force can be written as

$$D = \frac{1}{2} \rho A\, C_D V^2 ,$$

the presence of the ½ is a matter of convention. The direction of this force is such that it opposes the motion of the body and hence we may write

$$\mathbf{D} = -\frac{1}{2} \rho A\, C_D V^2\, \hat{\mathbf{V}} ,$$

where $\hat{\mathbf{V}}$ denotes a unit vector in the direction of the velocity V. The value of C_D lies in the range $[0, 1]$ and is dependent upon the body position adopted by the athlete. The more streamlined the position the lower the value of C_D.

The values of ρ at sea level and at the altitude of Mexico City are respectively

$$\rho_1 = 1.225 \text{ kgm}^{-3} \;\; ; \;\; \rho_2 = 0.984 \text{ kgm}^{-3} .$$

The body position adopted by a long jumper while in flight is not particularly streamlined and consequently the value of C_D is fairly high. A typical value would be $C_D \sim 0.75$ while a reasonable value for A would be $A \sim 0.75 \text{ m}^2$.

We are now in a position to solve the equation of motion and obtain an expression for the distance travelled by the long jumper during the time of flight. We can then evaluate the expression for the two different air densities and hence determine the difference in length of the jump. If, as we claim, air density effects are minimal then the calculated difference will be small.

Before attempting to solve the equation of motion

$$m\mathbf{a} = m\mathbf{g} - \frac{1}{2}\, \rho A\, C_D V^2\, \hat{\mathbf{V}}$$

we shall approximate the motion to the horizontal direction only. This is a reasonable assumption since the change in height of the centre of mass during the long jump is considerably less than the length of the jump. The horizontal component of the equation of motion is then

$$m\,\frac{\mathrm{d}u}{\mathrm{d}t} = -\frac{1}{2}\,\rho A\, C_D\, u^2$$

where u denotes the horizontal component of the velocity vector $\mathbf{V}$. Separating the variables and integrating this differential equation gives

$$\int_{u_0} \frac{\mathrm{d}u}{u^2} = -\frac{\rho A\, C_D}{2m} \int_0 \mathrm{d}t$$

$$\frac{1}{u} = \frac{\rho A\, C_D}{2m}\, t + \frac{1}{u_0}\,,$$

where u_0 denotes the athlete's take-off speed.

Since $u = \mathrm{d}x/\mathrm{d}t$ this last equation can be rewritten as

$$\frac{\mathrm{d}x}{\mathrm{d}t} = \frac{1}{\dfrac{1}{u_0} + \dfrac{\rho A\, C_D}{2m}\, t}\,.$$

Once again the variables can be separated and the equation integrated to obtain the distance travelled, R m, during the time of flight, T s.

$$\int_0^R \mathrm{d}x = \int_0^T \frac{\mathrm{d}t}{\dfrac{1}{u_0} + \dfrac{\rho A\, C_D}{2m}\, t}$$

$$R = \frac{2m}{\rho A\, C_D} \left[\log_e \left(\frac{1}{u_0} + \frac{\rho A\, C_D}{2m}\, t \right) \right]_0^T$$

$$= \frac{2m}{\rho A\, C_D} \log_e \left(1 + \frac{\rho A\, C_D u_0 T}{2m} \right)\,.$$

Reasonable values for the time of flight and the take-off velocity are 1 s and $10\ \text{ms}^{-1}$ respectively. Beamon himself weighed about 80 kg so

$$\frac{\rho A\, C_D u_0 T}{2m} \ll 1,$$

and the logarithmic term can be given its Maclaurin expansion as

$$R = \frac{2m}{\rho A\, C_D} \left\{ \frac{\rho A\, C_D u_0 T}{2m} - \frac{1}{2} \left(\frac{\rho A\, C_D u_0 T}{2m} \right)^2 + \ldots \right\}$$

$$\simeq u_0 T - \frac{\rho A\, C_D u_0{}^2}{4m}\ T^2.$$

If R_1 denotes the length of the jump at sea level (where the air density is ρ_1) and R_2 denotes the length at Mexico City (where the air density is ρ_2) then

$$R_2 - R_1 \simeq \frac{u_0{}^2 A\, C_D T^2}{4m}\ (\rho_1 - \rho_2)$$

$$= \frac{10^2 \times 0.75 \times 0.75 \times 1^2}{4 \times 80}\ (1.225 - 0.984)$$

$$= 0.042\ \text{m}\ .$$

Strictly speaking, the length of the long jump is $T + R + L$ but the values of T and L would be sensibly the same at both sea level and altitude as they only depend on the individual athlete. Thus it is valid to consider the difference $R_2 - R_1$. Since this is so small we conclude that Beamon's jump was indeed exceptional.

3.5 THE TRIPLE JUMP

The triple jump or, more correctly, the hop, step and jump, consists of an approach run, three 'jumps' and a final landing. The rules of international competition require that the first two jumps (the hop and the step) are made from the same leg, while the third jump is made from the other leg. Each of the three jumps can be categorized by the differences in their length, take-off angle and decreasing take-off speed. The basic technique for the event requires the athlete to attain a high velocity of approach and maintain horizontal momentum as much as possible during the three jump phases. A common fault amongst beginners is to make an enormous hop, thereby using up so much energy that they are subsequently unable to optimally perform the remaining two jump phases. The key word is 'optimally'; in the first two jump phases the athlete should concentrate on obtaining the optimum distance commensurate with retaining enough leg strength and efficiency to perform the final jump. Observation of many triple jumpers indicates that the ratio of the three phases hop:step:jump is of the order 4:3:4. Obviously, these figures vary from one athlete to another but they give an indication of the proportions necessary for an athlete to produce his best performance.

There are two main triple jump techniques conventionally recognized (the Polish and the Russian techniques, named after their country of origin). The Polish technique uses a low trajectory for the hop (thus covering less distance but conserving energy for the last two jumps). The Russian technique is based on a bounding action (which emphasizes height) and the hop is thus the longest of the three jumps. The question of which technique to adopt is resolved by considering the type of athlete involved. A sprinter should select the Polish technique whereas a light, strong-legged athlete should opt for the Russian technique. Whichever style is adopted, it is clear that a triple jumper must not only be a good sprinter but must possess great leg strength. This second attribute not only enables him to absorb the impacts of the intermediate landings but also to perform the successive take-offs under control.

The approach run

Most of the section on the approach run for the long jump is applicable to the triple jump too. Whatever approach technique is adopted the result must be the attainment of maximum controlled speed for take-off.

In view of the competition rules for this event, many athletes make the initial take-off from the stronger leg (as in the long jump) since this leg works twice. Some athletes prefer to use the weaker leg thus using the stronger leg for an all out take-off into the final jump.

The take-off

Whereas in the long jump the athlete's body is inclined backwards at the moment the foot is planted on the take-off board, the triple jumper's body is more vertical. This reduces the braking effect of the foot plant (thus conserving horizontal momentum) and enables the athlete's body to move faster over the take-off foot and drive off the board into the hop on a flight path which has a lower trajectory than for the long jump. If the drive off the board is directed too highly then too much speed is used up at take-off with obvious detrimental effects on the remaining phases.

In addition to ensuring that take-off is at a shallower angle than for the long jump, it is essential that the athlete is balanced at take-off. If he is not, then things will get progressively worse as the phases proceed, with the athlete needing to waste effort to regain balance instead of concentrating on achieving distance.

The hop

During the hop phase, after take-off, the legs perform a form of hitch kick action, as described in the long jump section. The landing is flat-footed (as are all triple jump landings in order to help absorb the considerable loads) with the landing foot ahead of the hips; not too far ahead or a braking effect is introduced. The arms are used to maintain the balance of the body during the hop.

The step

Having just absorbed the landing at the end of the hop, the take-off leg now extends again to initiate the step phase. The extended free leg, at this time trailing behind the body, is now bent at the knee and brought forwards quickly while the arms are driven backwards. The leg being brought forward is bent in order to reduce its moment of inertia about the hips and consequently to increase the angular speed of its rotation about the hips. During the step phase, there is a tendency for the trunk to rotate forwards. This is counteracted both by the arms and by the legs 'opening out' prior to landing. On landing, the foot must be ahead of the hips. The hips then move forward, over and ahead of the driving foot so that on take-off into the final jump the drive is applied behind the body's centre of mass (see also the long jump). The non-jumping leg is held back ready to swing strongly through, thus adding to the final jump. Lastly, both arms are swung rapidly forwards and upwards to assist the jump.

The jump

By the time this stage is reached it is likely that the athlete has lost so much forward momentum that any form of hitch kick is out of the question. It will thus be necessary to resort to the hang technique. The greater the horizontal speed the athlete can maintain, the better will be the final jump. On landing, the athlete's forward speed is less than in the long jump and the final throwing forwards of the arms (see the long jump) is essential in driving the body over the fulcrum of the feet. In some instances, so much horizontal speed has been lost that a skid landing, in which the athlete falls out to one side, may be unavoidable.

4

Fitness

4.1 ISOMETRIC ENDURANCE

When muscle varies in length upon activation the contraction is termed isotonic. Weight lifting and running are examples of isotonic exercise.

When both ends of the muscle are fixed and, though the muscle develops tension, no movement occurs in the joint involved the contraction is termed isometric. Holding a set of chest expanders open across the chest or pushing against an immovable object are examples of isometric exercise.

According to the standard definition of mechanical work done (work done = force × distance) there is therefore no work done in isometric exercises! Nevertheless, static work involves the expenditure of energy and can be extremely fatiguing, especially when the tension is high enough to prevent blood entering the muscle in which case the energy source is solely intramuscular. Many gymnasia are equipped with multi-station exercise machines, designed to exercise the various muscle groups of the body using both isotonic and isometric exercises.

The isometric exercises develop the body's muscular condition by using different muscle groups to resist a given load for a specified time interval. It is thus reasonable to ask whether there is a relationship between the load being resisted and the holding time.

The following experiment was designed by an exercise physiologist to investigate the above relationship for the knee extensor muscles (the muscles on the front of the thigh whose function is to extend the knee) of a group of male athletes. Each subject sat on a bench, with the legs together and the feet clear of the floor. The back of the bench was adjusted until the subject touched the seat of the bench with the back of the knees. The subject was allowed to grip the sides of the bench with the hands in order to avoid lifting himself off the bench as the load was applied. A harness was placed just above the ankle joint of one leg (each leg was exercised separately). The harness was attached by a cable leading back under the bench to the load which the subject was to resist. The seating position was set so that the angle between the upper and lower leg was a right angle (see Fig. 4.1). On the command 'Begin', the subject commenced to 'push' with the leg in order to resist the load. The time for which the load was

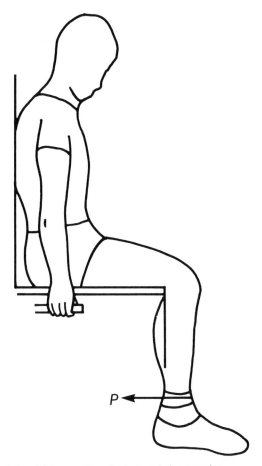

Fig. 4.1 – Seating position for isometric leg exercise.

resisted was measured. It should be emphasized that this is an isometric exercise, the leg does not actually move during the experiment.

After testing at a specific workload, a recovery time of three minutes was allowed before commencing the next workload. A typical set of results for one leg is given below.

Load (P kg)	Holding time (t s)
7	470
10	288
21	84
31	52
41	32

Figure 4.2 shows a graph of the data; clearly the relationship is not linear!

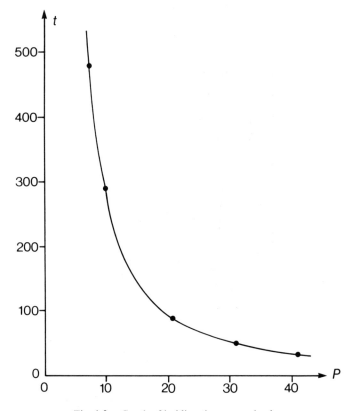

Fig. 4.2 – Graph of holding time versus load.

What do we do next in our attempt to determine the relationship between t and P? First we notice that the data span a considerable range. One way to reduce this span is to take logarithms of the data. Any base will do, we shall use the exponential number as the base. The result of taking natural logarithms of the data is the following revised table:

$\ln P$	$\ln t$
1.95	6.15
2.30	5.66
3.04	4.43
3.43	3.95
3.71	3.47

Notice how much more 'manageable' the data have become.

What graph shall we plot now? The answer is not clear; we really have no reason for presupposing that the relationship (if any) is exponential or of power form. Consequently, we must plot all the graphs possible using the two sets of data, i.e.

t versus $\ln P$,

$\ln t$ versus P, and

$\ln t$ versus $\ln P$.

Figure 4.3 shows these three graphs. It is evident that the graph of $\ln t$ versus $\ln P$ gives a good straight line. The data in the above table can be used as follows to obtain the equation of the straight line of best fit in the form:

$$\ln t = a + b \ln P$$

where

$$a = \frac{(\sum_i y_i)(\sum_i x_i^2) - (\sum_i x_i)(\sum_i x_i y_i)}{n \sum_i x_i^2 - (\sum_i x_i)^2} \, .$$

and

$$b = \frac{n \sum_i x_i y_i - (\sum_i x_i)(\sum_i y_i)}{n \sum_i x_i^2 - (\sum_i x_i)^2} \, ,$$

with $x_1 = 1.95, x_2 = 2.30, y_1 = 6.15, y_2 = 5.66$ etc., and $n = 5$.

Determining the various sums gives $a = 9.1334$ and $b = -1.5251$. The equation of the straight line is therefore

$$\ln t = 9.1334 - 1.5251 \ln P$$

from which the relationship between holding time and load is found to be

$$t = \frac{9259.45}{P^{1.5251}} \, . \tag{4.1}$$

The results used in this section are average results, obtained from a group of ten trained athletes. If you repeat the experiment you might obtain different values for the two parameters a and b.

Now that a theoretical model of the data has been obtained it is pertinent to ask 'how well does this least squares regression line fit the sample data?'. This question may be answered by determining the correlation coefficient r, for which $0 \leqslant r^2 \leqslant 1$,

$$r = \frac{n \sum_i x_i y_i - (\sum_i x_i)(\sum_i y_i)}{\sqrt{\left[n \sum_i x_i^2 - (\sum_i x_i)^2\right]\left[n \sum_i y_i^2 - (\sum_i y_i)^2\right]}} \, .$$

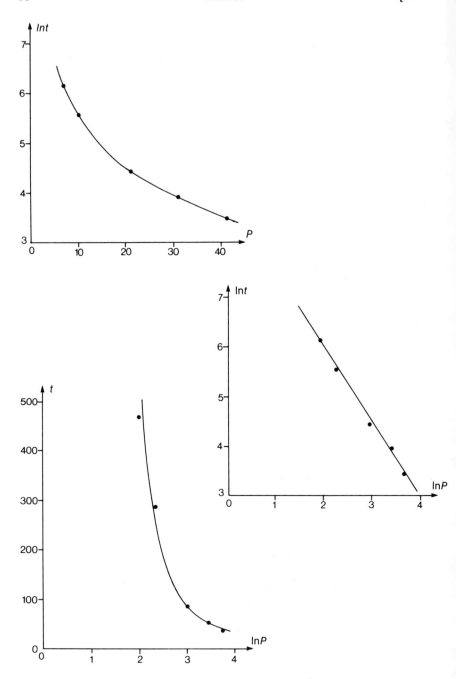

Fig. 4.3 – Graphical attempts to establish a $t - P$ relationship.

For the data used, $r = -0.9992$. This means that the relationship between holding time and load given by equation (4.1) fits the data very well indeed.

Although the above analysis has been performed on a small set of data, it illustrates the approach which can be adopted in order to investigate the relationship between holding time and load regardless of the sample size.

The method thus represents a valuable mathematical tool since once the existence of a holding time – load relationship has been established it may prove useful to the physiologist in the future.

4.2 HOW FIT ARE YOU? (HARVARD STEP TEST)

We have all heard people make derogatory remarks such as 'Huh! He's not very fit' about the the fitness of others.

One of the interests of exercise physiologists is the measurement of fitness. Before we examine one of the current measurement techniques we note the following two facts. The rate of a person's heart beat and the time required for that rate to return to normal upon cessation of exercise are partly determined by the person's physical condition. A person who is physically well-conditioned will also be less affected by a given amount of exercise than a poorly conditioned person. The fitter you are, the faster your pulse rate will return to normal after exercise. Since it is very easy to measure a person's pulse rate, many fitness tests have been developed which are based on a subject's pulse rate recovery after exercise.

These pulse ratio tests, as they are called, involve stepping up and down at a specified rate off a box of a specified height. One such test is the Harvard step test, so called since it was originally designed for use with male students at Harvard University in the United States of America. It is a very straightforward test to administer and consequently it has been adapted for groups of subjects other than male students. The values used for the height and rate are dependent upon the age and sex of the subjects since values suitable for an adult would be inappropriate for a child.

First the test for adult males is described, the modifications made for other age groups are given later. The subject steps up and down off a box 20 inches high at a rate of 30 times per minute. When the subject steps up onto the box he must attain a position in which the body is erect, crouching is not permittted. The stepping procedure involves four stages

(1) one foot placed on the box,
(2) other foot placed on the box,
(3) one foot placed on the floor,
(4) other foot placed on the floor.

The subject is permitted to change the order of the feet provided that the order of the four stages and the rate of stepping are maintained.

The stepping continues for 5 minutes unless exhaustion is reached previously! In either case, the duration of stepping is recorded.

Immediately after completion the subject sits down in a chair and three pulse counts are taken (at the wrist) at the following times

1 to 1½, 2 to 2½ and 3 to 3½ minutes

after stepping ceased.

The subject's Harvard Index is then obtained from the formula

$$\text{Harvard Index} = \frac{\text{Duration of exercise in seconds} \times 100}{2 \times (\text{sum of three pulse counts during recovery})} \cdot$$

The physical condition, or fitness, of the subject is then determined according to the following table

Harvard Index	Physical condition or level of fitness
> 90	Excellent
80–89	Good
55–79	Average
< 55	Poor

For example a Harvard step test using a highly trained marathon runner as a subject gave the following three pulse counts: 48, 46 and 44. The Harvard Index is therefore

$$\frac{300 \times 100}{2 \times (48 + 46 + 44)} = 108.7,$$

so we conclude that the subject was extremely fit. Marathon runners can be expected to score high values of the Harvard Index since the index is a measure of recovery from prolonged exercise and the marathon is certainly prolonged exercise!

Finally, a word of caution: this test is extremely arduous and should not be attempted unless you are sure that the subject is medically fit.

In order that you may determine your own Harvard Index or those of your colleagues the various modifications made to the standard test for subjects of different ages and sexes follow.

(i) Elementary school children (up to 12 years of age)
The height of the box is reduced to 14 inches and the duration of stepping is determined by the age of the child,

up to 7 years of age	2 minutes
8–12 years of age	3 minutes.

The scoring and classification are the same as for adult males.

(ii) Boys (12–17 years of age)
Between the ages of 12 and 17 a considerable range of sizes is observed in boys. This means that boxes of different heights should be used in the step test in order to make the test equally demanding for both small and large boys. The classification into small or large is made on the basis of body surface area, not simply the individual's height. The use of body surface area as the measure enables account to be taken of the subject's build as well as his height. The classification is as follows

if surface area < 1.85 m^2 then box height $= 18$ inches,
if surface area $\geqslant 1.85$ m^2 then box height $= 20$ inches.

This presents a problem – how do we find the surface area of the subject's body? To do this we use a nomogram. A nomogram is a chart or diagram of scaled lines or curves used to help in calculations. It consists of three scales in which a line joining values on two of the scales determines a third value. The body surface area nomogram is shown in Fig. 4.4 – the body surface area can be obtained from a knowledge of the height and weight of the subject. For example to obtain the body surface area of a youth who is 1.90 m tall and weighs 59 kg draw a straight line between the points 1.90 and 59 on the left- and right-hand scales respectively. The body surface area is then given by the intersection of this line with the centre line and is found to be 1.81 m^2.

    Once the appropriate box height has been determined the test and the three post-exercise pulse counts are conducted in the same way as for adult males, the only difference being that the duration of stepping is reduced to 4 minutes. Instead of determining the Harvard Index using the formula quoted earlier it is possible to use Table 4.1. The left-hand number of each pair in Table 4.1 represents the total pulse count and the right-hand number is the corresponding value of the Index. For example, if the total of the three pulse counts was 146 then the Index is found to be 82.

(iii) Girls (12–17 years of age)
The test is the same as for adult males except for a lower box, 16 inches high, and a reduced duration of stepping, 4 minutes. The total of the three post-exercise pulse counts is then used exactly as described for boys to obtain the value of the Index.

(iv) Women
The test is the same as for adult males except for a lower box, 18 inches high, and a reduced duration of stepping, 4 minutes. The total of the three post-exercise pulse counts is used in exactly the same way as for adult males to obtain the values of the Index.

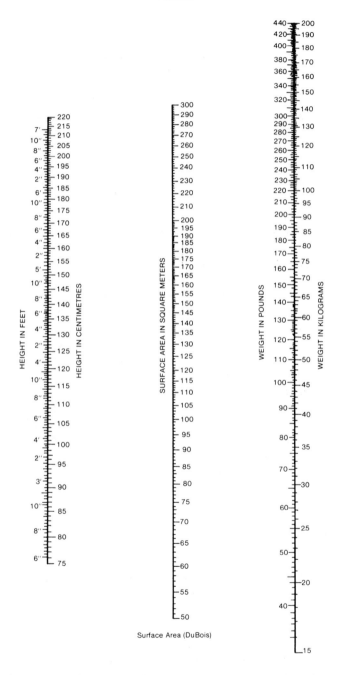

Surface Area (DuBois)

Fig. 4.4 – DuBois body surface chart: nomograph. Copyright 1920, by W. M. Boothby and R. B. Sandiford, Mayo Clinic, Rochester, Minn.

Table 4.1

Calculation of girls' physical efficiency index: modified Harvard step test

Pulse score	Pulse score	Pulse score	Pulse score
105–114	133–90	163–74	193–62
106–113	134–90	164–73	194–62
107–112	135–89	165–73	195–61
108–111	136–88	166–72	196–61
109–110	137–88	167–72	197–61
110–109	138–87	168–71	198–61
111–108	139–86	169–71	199–60
112–107	140–86	170–71	200–60
113–106	141–85	171–70	201–60
114–105	142–85	172–70	203–59
115–104	143–84	173–70	208–58
116–103	144–83	174–69	210–57
117–102	145–83	175–69	214–56
118–102	146–82	176–68	218–55
119–101	147–82	177–68	222–54
120–100	148–81	178–67	226–53
121–99	149–81	179–67	230–52
122–98	150–80	180–67	235–51
123–98	151–80	181–66	240–50
124–97	152–79	182–66	
125–96	153–78	183–66	
126–95	154–78	184–65	
127–95	155–77	185–65	
128–94	156–77	186–65	
129–93	158–76	189–64	
130–92	160–75	190–63	
131–92	161–75	191–63	
132–92	162–74	192–63	

Note: If pulse total is beyond limits of this table divide 120 by the pulse total to obtain the score.

Table 4.2 shows the Harvard Step Indices recorded by a group of English league footballers prior to, and on completion of, a one-month period of pre-season training. Common sense tells the manager that the players' fitness has improved but is there anything further which could be done to confirm his opinion?

Table 4.2

Harvard step index for a group of English league footballers during a one-month period of pre-season training

Subject number	1	2	3	4	5
Harvard Index (after)	82.3	102.5	98.7	102.0	98.7
Harvard Index (before)	72.1	87.7	81.9	85.7	83.3

Subject	6	7	8	9	10	11
H.I. (after)	94.3	93.8	100.0	89.8	97.4	98.0
H.I. (before)	73.5	75.7	80.7	75.3	78.9	78.1

Subject	12	13	14	15	16	17
H.I. (after)	125.0	92.0	104.9	89.3	111.0	94.9
H.I. (before)	71.7	70.4	68.5	71.4	83.8	82.4

Subject	18	19	20	21	22	23
H.I. (after)	100.6	115.4	102.0	119.8	96.1	124.7
H.I. (before)	84.5	84.4	78.5	90.3	87.2	83.5

Subject	24	25	26	27	28	29
H.I. (after)	99.3	93.2	74.6	88.7	119.0	75.7
H.I. (before)	77.3	84.5	58.8	79.8	80.6	71.1

Subject	30	31
H.I. (after)	104.9	94.3
H.I. (before)	81.5	88.2

This problem is an example of a situation in which statistical significance testing is useful. Since we are concerned with a 'before and after' effect we shall examine the differences, where difference is defined as

difference = Harvard Index after training − Harvard Index before training,

and because we are only interested in looking for an improvement in fitness we shall use a one-tailed test.

We shall use a t-test for which we shall require the mean and standard deviation of the differences. These are respectively

$$\bar{x} = 20.99 \text{ and } s_{n-1} = 11.69,$$

for the 31 subjects used. The t statistic is found from

$$t = \frac{\bar{x}}{s_{n-1}/\sqrt{n}}$$

to be

$$t = \frac{20.99 \times \sqrt{31}}{11.69} = 9.997.$$

The two levels of significance commonly used are the 5% and 1% levels which in the case of a one-tailed test and 30 degrees of freedom give the critical values of t as 1.697 and 2.457 respectively.

Our result is thus highly significant. As you probably anticipated there is a definite improvement in the fitness of the footballers as a result of their training programme. The manager can therefore conclude that he has a worthwhile training programme.

5

Miscellaneous Sports

5.1 OPTIMUM STRATEGY FOR POSITIONING OF OARSMEN

Introduction

When a traditionally rigged boat is propelled through the water, a small lateral oscillation of the stern of the boat is observed. This causes waves from alternate sides of the rudder which results in resistance to the motion of the boat, additional to the viscous and aerodynamic drag effects. This chapter contains a simple mechanical analysis which explains the reason for this oscillation. Some alternative rigging arrangements, which cause no oscillation, are presented.

Preliminary discussion

Consider the force F which an oar exerts on a boat through its point of contact, at the rowlock. This force can be resolved into its components P and N, parallel and normal to the direction of travel of the boat (see Fig. 5.1). Once the oar passes through the position $\theta = 90°$, the component N reverses its direction (see Fig. 5.2).

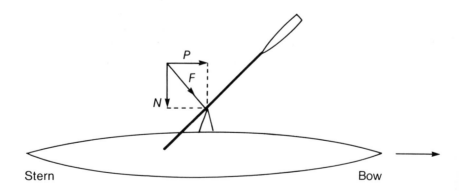

Stern   Bow

Fig. 5.1

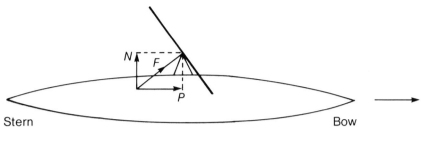

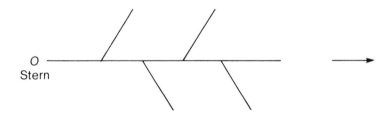

Fig. 5.2

Traditionally rigged four

For a traditionally rigged four, the arrangement of the oars is shown in Fig. 5.3.
Assume that each oarsman exerts the same force and let each of these be resolved
into its P and N components as explained previously.

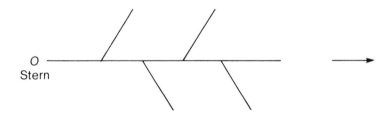

Fig. 5.3

Taking moments about any point on the centre line of the boat (for example
the stern, O) the total moment of the P forces is zero. If s denotes the distance
from the stern to the line of action of stroke's N force and l denotes the separation of the lines of action of the other oarsmens' N forces (see Fig. 5.4) then
taking moments about O, the total anticlockwise moment M_0 is given by

$$M_0 = -Ns + N(s + l) - N(s + 2l) + N(s + 3l) = 2Nl.$$

The effect of this is to cause the bow of the boat to move off course to the
left, as viewed from the stern. Once the oars reach positions for which $\theta > 90°$,
each of the components N reverses its direction and thus so does M_0. Hence the
bow moves off to the right. This continual change in the sign of M_0 causes the
observed oscillation of the stern.

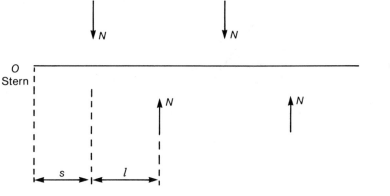

Fig. 5.4

An alternative rig – the Italian rig

In this section the above analysis is repeated for the Italian rig shown in Fig. 5.5. As before, the total moment of the P forces about the stern is zero. For this oar arrangement, the lines of action of the force components N are shown in Fig. 5.6. The total anticlockwise moment M_0 about the stern O is given by

$$M_0 = -Ns + N(s + l) + N(s + 2l) - N(s + 3l) = 0.$$

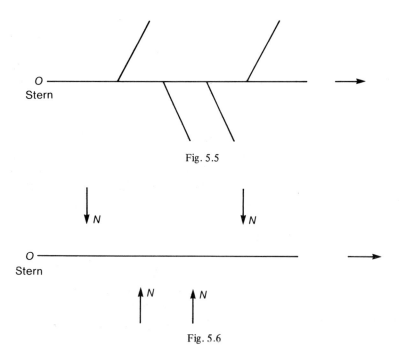

Fig. 5.5

Fig. 5.6

There is therefore no turning moment at any time during the stroke, and hence no 'weaving'.

The alternative rigging shown in Fig. 5.5 is therefore mechanically more efficient than the conventional rig which used to be seen at rowing regattas. This alternative rig is approved by the International Olympic Committee and, at international level, is now used more than the traditional one. One disadvantage of the Italian rig is that for the first few strokes after the start of a race it is difficult for the crew to drive the boat past the set of puddles caused by the previous stroke. Thus the oarsman nearest the stern can find himself rowing his first strokes in the rough water created by the man in the bow. Of course it is not essential to rerig a boat to overcome the problem of weaving. The effect can be reduced considerably by taking into account the strength and preference for rowing on a particular side of each crew member.

Other effects
The motion of a rowing boat is affected not only by the rig but also by factors such as the wind speed and direction. In a headwind the crew experiences an increase in wind resistance which slows them down. In addition, the wind causes waves which will not only increase the wetted area of the hull (and thus the viscous drag) but also makes it more difficult to row efficiently.

Tailwinds are not much better. A light tailwind will give some assistance but once the wind speed rises above approximately 3 ms^{-1} the water becomes rough and the waves cause problems as explained above.

Eights
A mechanically more efficient rig for a four has been discussed above. A similar analysis can be used to reveal the shortcomings in a traditionally rigged eight (see Fig. 5.7). Both the Italians and the Germans have developed alternative rigging arrangements for eights which reduce the 'weaving' moment to zero (see Fig. 5.8).

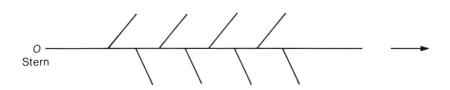

O
Stern

Fig. 5.7

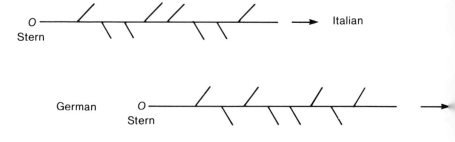

Fig. 5.8

5.2 THE NUMBER OF OARSMEN IN A BOAT

Introduction

Observation at a rowing regatta shows that the more oarsmen there are in a boat, the faster the boat travels. It is therefore reasonable to investigate whether there is a mathematical relationship between the speed of the boat, v, and the number of crew, n.

The mathematical model

The frictional drag, D, experienced by a boat travelling with speed v can be shown experimentally to be proportional to the square of the speed and also to the wetted surface area of the hull. The surface area of the hull is proportional to the product of the length and beam of the boat. Generally speaking the longer the boat, the broader the beam and thus the surface area of the hull is proportional to the square of the length. Combining these two results gives

$$D \propto v^2 \, l^2. \qquad (5.1)$$

The volume of the boat can be considered to be proportional to l^3 and also, it might reasonably be supposed, to the number of crew, n. Hence

$$l^3 \propto n,$$

so

$$l \propto n^{1/3}. \qquad (5.2)$$

Equations (5.1) and (5.2) can be combined to give

$$D \propto v^2 \, n^{2/3}. \qquad (5.3)$$

The total power exerted by the crew in overcoming the drag is given by vD which is thus proportional to $v^3 \, n^{2/3}$. If each oarsman is assumed to supply an amount P then $nP \propto v^3 \, n^{2/3}$, from which

$$v \propto n^{1/9}.$$

Verification of the model
The validity of the above result can be tested using the results of the finals of the rowing events at the 1980 Olympics, for which the length of the course was 2000 m. The table gives the time taken, T s, and the number of oarsmen in the crew, n.

n	T
1	429.61
2	408.01
4	368.17
8	349.05

(With the exception of the eight, all the results refer to coxless crews. The result quoted for the $n = 2$ case is for the coxless pair (one oar per man) as opposed to the double scull (two oars per man)).

A plot of log T versus log n shows that a straight line of slope -0.11 fits the data well, thus establishing that

$$T \propto n^{-0.11}.$$

Since $v \propto T^{-1}$ then $v \propto n^{0.11}$, which gives good agreement with the result predicted earlier.

Do passengers make a difference?
Many of the rowing events take place with, and without, a cox. It is interesting to speculate whether the result $v \propto n^{1/9}$ is significantly changed if the results for coxed crews are used instead of those for coxless crews. The corresponding results for crews carrying a cox are given for you to analyse.

n	T
1	429.61
2	422.54
4	374.51
8	349.05

(The result quoted for the $n = 2$ case is for the coxed pair as opposed to the double scull.)

You will notice that the times for coxed crews are inferior to those for coxless crews. This suggests that it is better to have the crew responsible for both steering and propulsion rather than to have more accurate steering and incur a weight penalty by carrying the cox.

5.3 DOWNHILL SKIING

In downhill skiing the primary objective is to achieve as high a velocity as possible in order to minimize the time taken to cover the course.

Various factors have been considered in this quest for greater speed. Ski waxes have been developed to a very great extent, a typical value for the coefficient of friction between the skis and the snow is now as low as 0.05, while ski clothing now fits like a second skin and is made from very smooth materials.

More recently, some of the world's leading skiers have experimented with slight increases in the mass of the skier—ski system and found that this too increases the terminal velocity down the slope.

To understand why, it is only necessary to consider a simple model of the forces acting on a skier as he skis down a slope of uniform gradient, while adopting a fixed body position.

The forces considered are the skier's weight (mg), the frictional force (F) between the skis and the slope and the aerodynamic drag force (D) caused by the cross-sectional area which the skier's body presents to the air, see Fig. 5.9.

If μ denotes the coefficient of sliding friction between the skis and the snow then

$$F = \mu\, mg \cos \alpha. \tag{5.4}$$

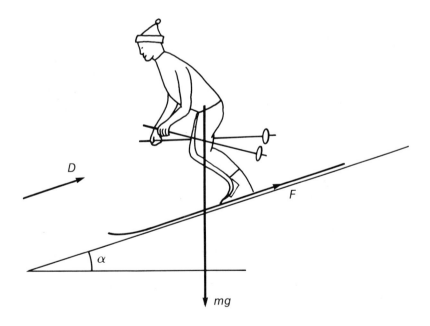

Fig. 5.9 – Forces acting on a downhill skier.

Applying Newton's second law of motion down the line of the slope then gives

$$ma = mg \sin \alpha - \mu \, mg \cos \alpha - D \,, \tag{5.5}$$

where a denotes the skier's acceleration down the slope.

The drag force D experienced by the skier has the same form as that introduced earlier for the long jumper, i.e.

$$D = \frac{1}{2} \, \rho \, A \, C_D \, v^2 \,. \tag{5.6}$$

Since the body position adopted by a downhill skier is more streamlined than that of the long jumper then the values of A and C_D will be less. The terminal velocity $(\overline{V})$ of the skier is attained once his acceleration becomes zero so that, from equation (5.5),

$$D = mg \sin \alpha - \mu \, mg \cos \alpha.$$

Equating the two expressions for D then gives the terminal velocity of the skier as

$$\overline{V} = \sqrt{\left\{ \frac{2mg \, (\sin \alpha - \mu \cos \alpha)}{\rho \, A \, C_D} \right\}}. \tag{5.7}$$

Some typical values of the various parameters involved in equation (5.7) are

$$m = 80 \text{ kg (clothed skier plus skis)}$$

$$\alpha = 15°$$

$$A = 0.6 \text{ m}^2$$

$$C_D = 0.7$$

$$\mu = 0.05$$

$$\rho = 1.25 \text{ kg m}^{-3},$$

so that taking $g = 9.81$ ms^{-2} the terminal velocity of the skier is

$$\overline{V} = 25.09 \text{ ms}^{-1}.$$

The velocity as a function of displacement (s) down the slope may be found from equation (5.5) by first writing it as

$$mv \, \frac{dv}{ds} + \frac{1}{2} \, \rho \, A \, C_D v^2 = mg \sin \alpha - \mu \, mg \cos \alpha$$

and then recognizing that this can be expressed in the form

$$\frac{d}{ds} \left(\frac{1}{2} v^2 \right) + \frac{\rho \, A \, C_D}{m} \cdot \frac{1}{2} \, v^2 = g(\sin \alpha - \mu \cos \alpha) \tag{5.8}$$

Equation (5.8) is of integrating factor type with an integrating factor given by

$$\exp\left(\int \frac{\rho A C_D}{m} \, ds\right) = \exp\left(\frac{\rho A C_D \, s}{m}\right).$$

Multiplying equation (5.8) by the integrating factor then gives

$$\frac{d}{ds}\left\{\frac{1}{2} v^2 \exp\left(\frac{\rho A C_D}{m} \cdot s\right)\right\} = g(\sin \alpha - \mu \cos \alpha) \cdot \exp\left(\frac{\rho A C_D}{m} \cdot s\right) \quad (5.9)$$

If it is now assumed that the skier starts from rest at $s = 0$ and has a velocity v after a displacement s down the slope then integration of equation (5.9) gives

$$v^2 = \frac{2mg(\sin \alpha - \mu \cos \alpha)}{\rho A C_D} \cdot \left[1 - \exp\left(-\frac{\rho A C_D \, s}{m}\right)\right].$$

Using equation (5.7), the velocity v at displacement s can be expressed in terms of the terminal velocity $\bar{V}$ as

$$v(s) = \bar{V} \cdot \sqrt{\left\{1 - \exp\left(-\frac{\rho A C_D s}{m}\right)\right\}}. \quad (5.10)$$

If this equation is written as a differential equation

$$\frac{ds}{dt} = \bar{V} \cdot \sqrt{\left\{1 - \exp\left(-\frac{\rho A C_D s}{m}\right)\right\}}$$

then separating the variables and integrating gives

$$\int_0^s \frac{ds}{\sqrt{(1 - \exp(-ks))}} = \bar{V} \int_0^t dt, \quad (5.11)$$

where $k = \rho A C_D/m$. Completion of this integration will give a relationship between the elapsed time (t) and the distance travelled down the slope (s). The integration is simplified by means of the substitution

$$z^2 = 1 - \exp(-ks)$$

and the resulting expression for the elapsed time is

$$t = \frac{1}{k\bar{V}} \ln\left(\frac{1 + z}{1 - z}\right). \quad (5.12)$$

For the data introduced earlier, $k = 0.0066$ so that for a 2500 m segment of a downhill ski run the elapsed time is 108 s, using $\bar{V} = 25.09 \text{ ms}^{-1}$. The downhill skier is always striving to improve his velocity, or equivalently his elapsed time, over a course. Equations (5.10) and (5.12) show that this is equivalent to improving the terminal velocity ($\bar{V}$); thus any strategies for improvement can be determined by considering $\bar{V}$ itself. From equation (5.7), the parameters over which the skier has some measure of control are μ, A, C_D and m. As far as the first two of these parameters are concerned, there is not much scope for any major improvement. Ski waxes have already been developed to a very high standard and until some new product is developed which drastically reduces the value of μ there is unlikely to be any major improvement in $\bar{V}$.

A similar situation exists with regard to the cross-sectional area (A) which the skier presents to the air. Many countries already submit their most talented downhill skiers to a series of experiments in a wind tunnel in order to determine the body position, the so called egg position, which minimizes A. The drag force D is also influenced by the material and fit of the ski suit; a figure hugging suit will offer less resistance to the air than a loosely flapping coat. Racing ski suits do in fact fit like a second skin and so the only possible area for development is to make the suits of a more 'slippy' material. Any such improvements are limited by rules and safety considerations.

The most promising area of development for improving terminal velocity is thus seen to be a small increase in the mass of the skier and his skis. The increase has to be small since otherwise any benefits might be offset by adversely affecting the skier's body position and stability. If the small mass increase is denoted by δm and the corresponding increase in terminal velocity by $\delta \bar{V}$ then, assuming that all the other parameters are kept constant

$$\frac{\delta \bar{V}}{\delta m} \simeq \frac{d\bar{V}}{dm}.$$

From equation (5.7)

$$\frac{d\bar{V}}{dm} = \frac{g(\sin \alpha - \mu \cos \alpha)}{\bar{V} \rho A C_D}$$

so that

$$\delta \bar{V} \simeq \frac{\delta m.g(\sin \alpha - \mu \cos \alpha)}{\bar{V} \rho A C_D}.$$

Using the data introduced earlier, a 1% increase in m produces an increase in terminal velocity of 0.13 ms^{-1}, causing an improvement in the elapsed time for the 2500 m run of 0.54 s. At the highest levels of competition, such an improvement could make the difference between being first and being nowhere! The mass increase is usually effected by weighting the skis. It is interesting to note that skiers with higher body densities would have an inherent advantage, since for a given body size such a skier would have a greater mass and thus a higher terminal velocity, without incurring any penalty due to an increase in cross-sectional area A. Perhaps, in future high body density may become a prerequisite for selection to a downhill ski squad!

5.4 ONE HUNDRED AND EIGHTY! – OR LESS

The maximum score which a darts player can attain with one dart is 60 (a treble 20). Top-class players possess the ability to reproduce this score almost at will. For players of more average ability, achieving a treble 20 is a much rarer occurrence. It follows therefore that actually aiming at the treble 20 may not be the best strategy for such a player. Perhaps a better strategy would be to aim higher in the '20' region in order to reduce the chances of falling into the '1' or the '5' regions on either side?

In order to investigate this, a player of average ability was asked to record the results of three hundred throws for each of the following strategies:

(1) Aim at A, (see Fig. 5.10),
(2) Aim at B,
(3) Aim at C.

The results are given in Table 5.1.

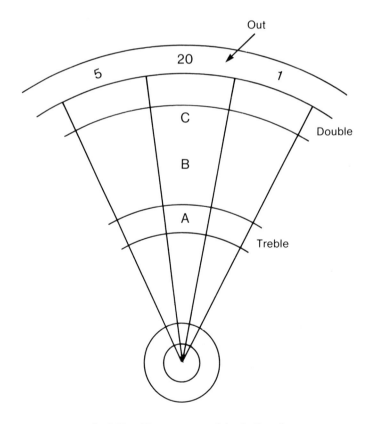

Fig. 5.10 – The target area of the dartboard.

Table 5.1

Strategy	Single 20	Double 20	Treble 20	Single 5	Double 5	Treble 5	Single 1	Double 1	Treble 1	Out
1	87	0	33	69	0	24	66	0	21	0
2	144	18	12	57	3	6	51	3	6	0
3	123	57	0	33	15	0	30	12	0	30

Table 5.2

Strategy	Single 20	Double 20	Treble 20	Single 5	Double 5	Treble 5	Single 1	Double 1	Treble 1	Out
1	0.29	0	0.11	0.23	0	0.08	0.22	0	0.07	0
2	0.48	0.06	0.04	0.19	0.01	0.02	0.17	0.01	0.02	0
3	0.41	0.19	0	0.11	0.05	0	0.10	0.04	0	0.10

The laws of probability may be applied to these data to answer simple questions such as

(a) What is the probability of a single dart falling in the ten different zones for each of the three strategies?

Pr $\{$single 20$\}$ = 87/300 = 0.29, using strategy (1)
Pr $\{$double 5$\}$ =   3/300 = 0.01, using strategy (2)
Pr $\{$double 20$\}$ = 57/300 = 0.19, using strategy (3).

The complete set of probabilities is given in Table 5.2

(b) For each of the three strategies, what is the probability that a single dart scores twenty or more?
Using strategy (1)

Pr $\{$a single dart scores twenty or more$\}$ = 0.29 + 0 + 0.11 = 0.40.

Using strategy (2)

Pr $\{$a single dart scores twenty or more$\}$ = 0.48 + 0.06 + 0.04 = 0.58.

Using strategy (3)

Pr $\{$a single dart scores twenty or more$\}$ = 0.41 + 0.19 + 0 = 0.60.

(c) A 'throw' is defined to be the throwing of three darts. What is the probability that each dart in a 'throw' scores twenty or more?
Using strategy (1)

Pr $\{$each dart in a 'throw' scores twenty or more$\}$ = $(0.40)^3$ = 0.064

Using strategy (2)

Pr{each dart in a 'throw' scores twenty or more} $= (0.58)^3 = 0.195$.

Using strategy (3)

Pr{each dart in a 'throw' scores twenty or more} $= (0.60)^3 = 0.216$.

(d) What is the probability that the score from a 'throw' is one hundred and twenty or more?

The various ways in which a score of at least one hundred and twenty or more can be achieved are

	40	40	40	or,
6 arrangements of	60	40	20	or,
3 arrangements of	60	40	40	or,
3 arrangements of	60	60	any.	

The probability of each of these arrangements is calculated for the various strategies using the data of Table 5.2. For example, using strategy (2)

$\text{Pr}\{60, 40, 20\} = 0.04 \times 0.06 \times 0.48 = 0.001152$.

Using strategy (2)

Pr{any score} $= 1$ (since Pr{out} $= 0$).

Thus

$\text{Pr}\{60, 60, \text{any}\} = 0.04 \times 0.04 \times 1 = 0.0016$.

Using strategy (3)

Pr{any score} $= 0.9$ (since Pr{out} $= 0.1$).

Thus

$\text{Pr}\{60, 60, \text{any}\} = 0 \times 0 \times 0.9 = 0$.

The complete set of results is given in Table 5.3.

Table 5.3

Event	Strategy(1)	Strategy (2)	Strategy (3)
Pr{40,40,40}	0	0.000216	0.00686
6Pr{60,40,20}	0	0.006912	0
3Pr{60,40,40}	0	0.000432	0
3Pr{60,60,any}	0.0363	0.004800	0
Totals	0.0363	0.01236	0.00686

Thus, if a player wishes to score at least one hundred and twenty he would be best advised to adopt strategy (1) when he could expect a success rate of about 1 in 30.

The average score per dart is defined to be

$$\sum_{\text{scores}} (\text{probability of score} \times \text{score})$$

Using this definition, it is possible to determine the strategy which our player should adopt if his objective is to maximize his score each 'throw'.

The average score per 'throw' = 3 × average score per dart

$$= 3 \sum_{\text{score}} (\text{prob. of score} \times \text{score})$$

For strategy (1) this gives

$$3 \times \{20 \times .29 + 40 \times 0 + 60 \times .11 + 5 \times .23 + 10 \times 0 + 15 \times .08 + 1 \times .22$$
$$+ 2 \times 0 + 3 \times .07\} = 45.54.$$

Similarly, for strategy (2) the average score per throw = 48 and for strategy (3) the average score per throw = 51.09.

Thus strategy (3) is the best one to adopt if the player wishes to maximize his score with each 'throw'.

5.5 ICE SKATING, GYMNASTICS AND HIGHBOARD DIVING

In each of the above sports, the participant rotates about an axis which is either internal or external to the body. This axis of rotation may be fixed as in the case of a gymnast performing Great Circles and an ice-skater spinning about his vertical axis, or its position may vary as in the case of a somersaulting diver or trampolinist.

In order to answer questions such as 'Why does a spinning ice-skater, with arms outstretched, speed up as the arms are brought down to the sides?' and 'Why is it important for a somersaulting diver or gymnast to "tuck well in"'?', it is necessary to consider the angular momentum of the athlete. This requires a biomechanical model of the athlete. While it is realized that an athlete is an extremely complex biomechanical system, it is possible to obtain useful information about the mechanical aspects of various athletic activities by considering a simple model based on a system of circular cylinders. In this, the athlete is considered to be a system of five circular cylinders: two legs, two arms and a combined head and torso, see Fig. 5.11. To describe the angular momentum of a rigid rotating body, such as this cylindrical athlete, requires the concept of moment of inertia, I. The moment of inertia of a body about a given axis is defined as

$$I = \Sigma mr^2$$

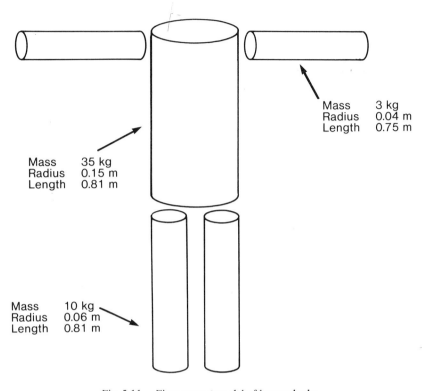

Fig. 5.11 − Five-segment model of human body.

where the summation takes place over all the particles which comprise the rigid body, see Fig. 5.12. It is thus a measure of the mass of the body and its distribution about the axis.

Before we attempt to answer the questions posed earlier in this section some preliminary results are necessary. These are:

(i) the moment of inertia of a circular cylinder of mass m, radius a and length l rotating about either its longitudinal axis or about an axis through its centre of mass and perpendicular to its length (see Fig. 5.13)

$$I_{XX'} = m\left(\frac{a^2}{4} + \frac{l^2}{12}\right), \quad I_{YY'} = \frac{ma^2}{2} \quad .$$

(ii) the parallel axes theorem which states that if a rigid body is rotating about an axis through some point O about which its moment of inertia is I_O and if I_G denotes the moment of inertia of the body about a parallel axis through the centre of mass, G, then

$$I_O = I_G + mh^2,$$

where m is the mass of the body and h is the perpendicular distance between the two axes (see Fig. 5.14).

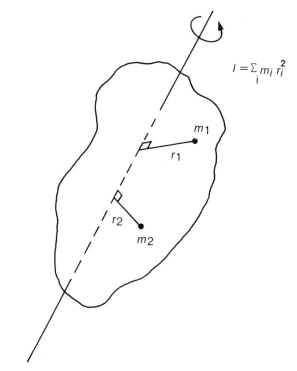

$$I = \sum_i m_i \, r_i^2$$

Fig. 5.12

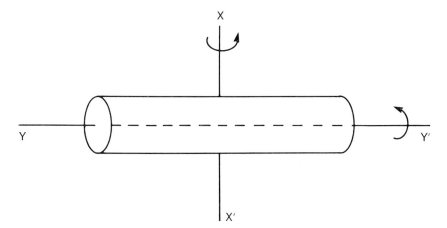

Fig. 5.13 – Cylinder axes used in determination of moment of inertia.

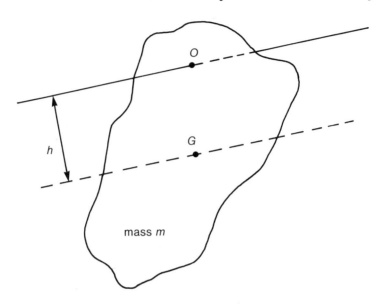

Fig. 5.14 – Parallel axes theorem $I_O = I_G + mh^2$.

The spinning ice-skater
In this section an analysis is presented which explains why the angular speed of rotation of an ice-skater rotating about a fixed vertical axis increases as the arms are brought from their initial outstretched position down to the sides. The initial and final configuration of the body are shown in Fig. 5.15 where YY′ represents the axis of rotation of the skater.

For both configurations,

I_{torso}, about axis of rotation YY′ $= 35(0.15)^2/2 = 0.3938$.

I_{leg}, about axis ZZ′ $= 10(0.06)^2/2 = 0.0180$,

so using the parallel axes theorem

$\qquad I_{leg}$, about axis of rotation YY′ $= 0.0180 + 10(0.09)^2 = 0.0990$.

In the arms outstretched position

$$I_{arm}, \text{ about axis XX}' = 3\left(\frac{0.04^2}{4} + \frac{0.75^2}{12}\right) = 0.1418.$$

Since the arm is rotating about YY′ then, using the parallel axes theorem,

$\qquad I_{arm}$, about axis of rotation YY′ $= 0.1418 + 3(0.375 + 0.15)^2 = 0.9687$.

In the arms by sides position

$\qquad I_{arm}$, about axis WW′ $= 3(0.04)^2/2 = 0.0024$,

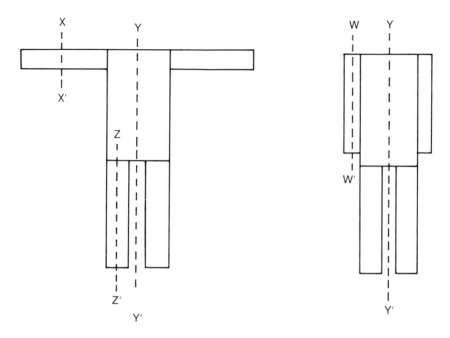

Fig. 5.15 – Initial and final body positions of ice-skater.

and since the arm is rotating about YY′ then

I_{arm}, about axis of rotation YY′ $= 0.0024 + 3(0.04 + 0.15)^2 = 0.1107$.

In the arms outstretched position the total moment of inertia of skater about the axis of rotation is

$$I = 0.3938 + 2 \times 0.0990 + 2 \times 0.9687 = 2.5292,$$

while with arms by sides

$$I = 0.3938 + 2 \times 0.0990 + 2 \times 0.1107 = 0.8132.$$

Suppose that with arms outstretched the skater's angular speed is 2.5 revolutions per second then his angular momentum is

$$Iw = 2.5292 \times 2.5 = 6.323$$

If after bringing the arms down to the sides, the new angular speed is w revolutions per second then the angular momentum is

$$Iw = 0.8132 \, w.$$

Applying the principle of conservation of angular momentum gives

$$0.8132 \, w = 6.323$$

whence

$$w = 7.78 \text{ rev/s},$$

illustrating that the angular speed of the skater increases considerably when the arms are moved down to the sides.

In practice, ice-skaters bring their arms in and across the front of their body. Since this has the effect·of bringing the mass of the arms even closer to the axis of rotation it would reduce the moment of inertia below the above value of 0.8132. The only difference this would make would be to increase the final angular speed still further above its value of 7.78 rev/s.

We have not analysed this more realistic final body position since the determination of the associated moment of inertia is made considerably more complicated by the need to model each arm as two cylinders (upper and lower arm) and locate their centres of mass once the arms are folded across the body.

You may wonder why the kinetic energy of rotation ($\frac{1}{2} I w^2$) with arms out has not been equated with that for arms by sides (using the principle of conservation of energy) in order to determine the increase in angular speed. Quite simply it is because such an equation would be incorrect, since as the arms are lowered to the sides there is a reduction in their potential energy. Consequently it is easier to examine the angular momentum of the skater.

The somersaulting gymnast or diver

It is apparent from the definition of moment of inertia given earlier that if the various particles of the body are grouped close to the axis of rotation then the value of the moment of inertia will be less than that when some of the particles are further away from the axis of rotation.

Figure 5.16 illustrates the various attitudes attained by a gymnast, or diver, performing a forward one-and-a-half-somersault (in each case the dot indicates the position of the instantaneous axis of rotation). At stage (i) the athlete possesses both linear and angular momentum. The linear momentum is needed to project him high into the air, in order to give him time for his angular momentum to enable him to complete his somersault.

It is desirable for the athlete to have a high angular momentum in order that he can complete his somersault quickly and have time to prepare for landing, or entering the water.

In stages (ii), (iii) and (iv) the athlete is 'tucking in' his mass as closely as possible about the axis of rotation. This will cause I to have a smaller value than in the extended position (i), since $I = \Sigma m r^2$. Consequently the angular speed of rotation, w, will be higher because of the principle of conservation of angular momentum and the fact that angular momentum = $I w$.

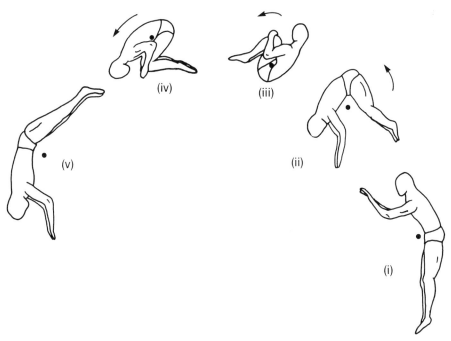

Fig. 5.16 – Forward one-and-a-half somersault.

At stage (v) the somersault has been performed and the athlete begins to extend his body, thereby increasing the value of I and so reducing w, prior to completion of the exercise.

Novice gymnasts instinctively use these results when they 'tuck' in preparation for landing from a handspring. They realize that they may have insufficient angular momentum to enable the exercise to be completed elegantly, so they 'tuck'. This increases their angular velocity so that at least they avoid the embarrassment of landing on their back!

6

Sailing

6.1 GENERAL DISCUSSION OF AERO- AND HYDRODYNAMIC PHENOMENA IN SAILING

It may seem strange to begin a chapter on sailing with a discussion on how an aircraft becomes airborne. Nevertheless the lift force that causes an aircraft to rise off the ground has the same origin as the force which drives a sailing vessel. Fig. 6.1(a) shows the airflow around a vertical cross-section of an aircraft wing which is inclined at a small angle of incidence to the undisturbed incident flow. Notice that the airflow separates from the wing surface and can become turbulent as it nears the trailing edge. This phenomenon will be returned to later in the chapter.

In order to understand the phenomenon of lift we must accept a result due to Bernoulli which links together the pressure p, the speed u and the density ρ at any point of the medium in which the flow occurs through the equation

$$p + \frac{1}{2} \rho u^2 = \text{constant.}$$

In Fig. 6.1(a) the streamlines are closer together above the wing than they are below it; consequently the air velocity is greater above the wing than below it. (The streamlines can be interpreted in the same way as the isobars on a weather chart: the closer they are together the stronger the wind.) If the suffix A refers to values above the wing and B refers to values below it then Bernoulli's theorem implies that

$$p_A + \frac{1}{2} \rho_A u_A^2 = p_B + \frac{1}{2} \rho_B u_B^2 .$$

If we assume that the medium in which the flow occurs is incompressible then since $u_A > u_B$ we find that

$$p_A < p_B .$$

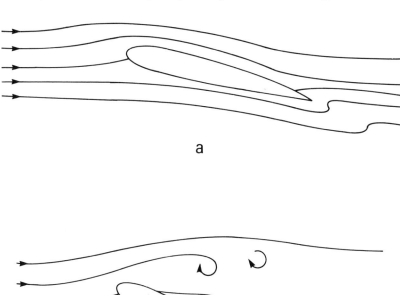

a

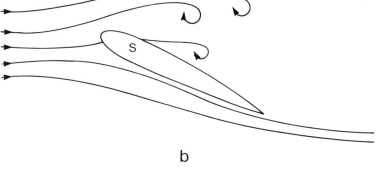

b

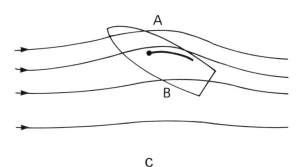

c

Fig. 6.1 − (a) Airflow around aerofoil section at small angle of incidence. (b) Airflow around aerofoil section at large angle of incidence to show stalling action. (c) Plan view of airflow around yacht sail.

This pressure difference between the upper and lower surfaces of the wing causes a resultant thrust to act vertically upwards on the wing. Fig. 6.1(c) shows a plan view of a sailing dinghy rigged with a single sail together with an indication of the wind direction. The shape of any horizontal cross-section of the sail is similar to the profile of the aerofoil. Hence the sail experiences a force acting in the direction BA, just like the aerofoil of Fig. 6.1(a). The driving force experienced by the sailing vessel is then given by the component of this force which acts in the direction of motion.

The pressure distribution across the width of the sail can be measured experimentally in a wind tunnel by connecting a manometer to different parts and/or sides of the sail as shown in Fig. 6.2(a). It is customary to plot the relative pressure intensity against the percentage of chord length, measured from the mast, where

$$\text{Relative Pressure Intensity} = \frac{P - Q}{\frac{1}{2} \rho u^2} ,$$

P = pressure measured by the manometer at the sail, Q = atmospheric pressure in the undisturbed flow, and u = air velocity.

Fig. 6.2(b) shows a typical pressure plot. In particular it is seen that there is a sudden drop in pressure after the mast, especially on the leeward (sheltered) side. This pressure drop, which accounts for most of the aerodynamic force on the sail, is explained by the viscous effects of the airflow past the mast. Ideally when a fluid such as air flows past a cylindrical boundary the resultant flow pattern is not the symmetric one shown in Fig. 6.3(a) except in the case of slow flows. Instead the airflow separates from the boundary after passing the points C and D (called separation points) and forms a wake which can become turbulent, see Fig. 6.3(b). The pressure in the wake immediately downstream of the mast is then less than it is upstream. A similar phenomenon is employed to advantage by racing car drivers who endeavour to get into a position immediately behind an opponent since the reduced air pressure (and consequently reduced resistance forces) encountered there means that subsequently they will have some power available with which to pull out and accelerate past their opponent at the last minute.

From Fig. 6.2(b) it is seen that the highest pressures, and therefore the greatest aerodynamic forces, correspond to the foreparts of the sail. As we move across the sail towards the stern we pass first through positions where the pressure only contributes a side force on the sail (causing undesirable leeway) and then to a position where the driving force may even be directed astern, see Fig. 6.4.

Fig. 6.3(c) shows that the presence of the mast has a disturbing effect on the airflow over the sail although obviously you cannot get rid of the mast; something is needed to support the sail. The majority of yachts are rigged with

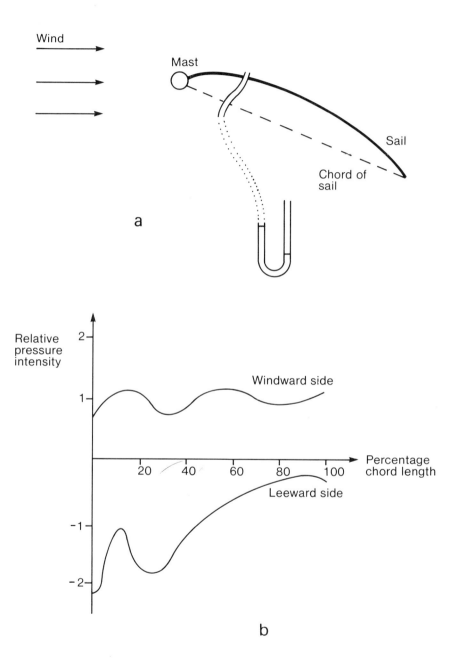

Fig. 6.2 – Pressure distribution over sail.

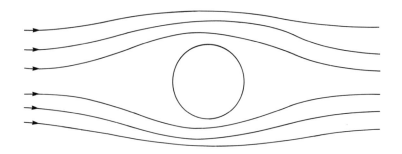

a

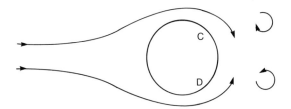

b

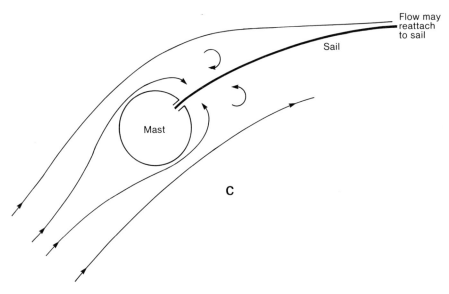

c

Fig. 6.3 – (a) Symmetric flow pattern of perfect fluid past an obstacle. (b) Actual flow pattern, showing separation at C, D and wake. (c) Air flow around cylindrical mast and sail.

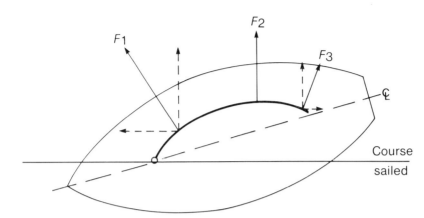

Fig. 6.4 – Aerodynamic contributions to the propulsive force: useful from F_1, nil from F_2 and detrimental from F_3.

a second, smaller sail called the jib which is located forward of the mainsail. The jib is not attached to a mast but to a rope or wire, called the forestay, which runs from the bow to the top of the mast. The absence of a mast intruding into the airflow enables a much smoother airflow to be obtained around the jib to the extent that the jib can be up to twice as efficient as the mainsail. Apart from the obvious advantage of providing an additional driving force, the jib is used in conjunction with the mainsail to improve the airflow, and hence the aerodynamic force, around the mainsail and delay the onset of separation on the mainsail. The two sails work together in exactly the same way as slotted wings which are used to promote laminar (smooth) flow over the wings of aircraft (see Fig. 6.5).

Now that the origin of the yacht's motive force has been discussed we must consider the stability of the yacht and investigate the consequences of the fact that generally a yacht sails at some angle of heel, θ, to the vertical. For this we shall restrict our attention to a yacht which is sailing to windward since this is generally

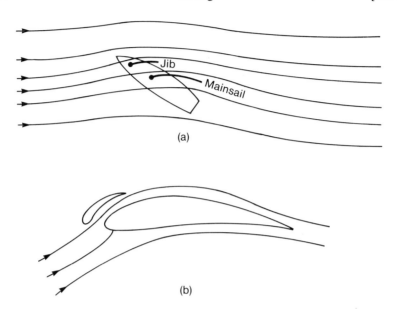

Fig. 6.5 – (a) Improvement in flow pattern using combination of jib and mainsail.
(b) Cross-section of slotted wing.

considered to be the most important aspect of a yacht's performance. Fig. 6.6
shows the resolution of the aerodynamic force A, acting on a single sail at its
centre of pressure C, into its driving and heeling components (The centre of
pressure is defined to be the point at which the application of a single force has
the same effect as the total aerodynamic force on the sail. For those readers
familiar with double integration, calculation of the position of the centre of
pressure is presented later in this chapter in the section on windsurfing.) The
heeling component can then be resolved into its horizontal and vertical components. The unbalancing effect of the aerodynamically caused heeling force is
countered by the total hydrodynamic force exerted by the water on the keel
this being assumed to act at the centre of pressure E of the keel. The heeling
moment is defined as

$$\text{heeling moment} = F_H \times h$$

where h is the distance between C and E as shown in Fig. 6.6.

The effect of the vertical component of the heeling force is to depress the
hull further into the water and hence to increase the wetted area of the hull
which we shall see later leads to an increased hydrodynamic resistance. It can
also alter the angle of incidence of the sail relative to the wind. Together with
the driving force, the vertical component of the heeling force can also affect the
fore and aft trim of the yacht.

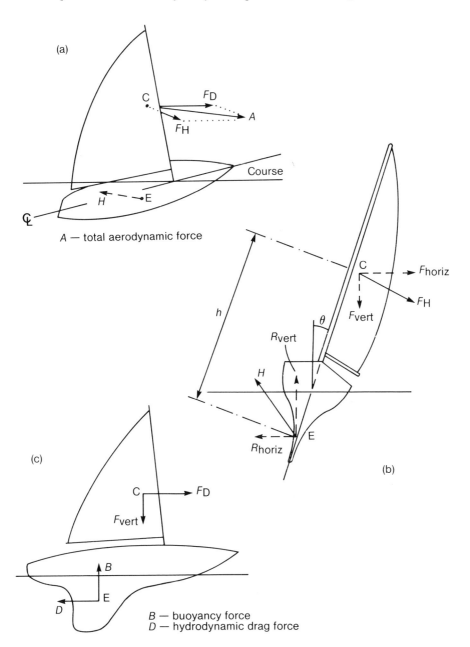

(a)

F_D

F_H

C

A

Course

H

E

$\mathbb{C}_L$

A — total aerodynamic force

(b)

h

θ

C

F_{horiz}

F_H

F_{vert}

R_{vert}

H

E

R_{horiz}

(c)

C

F_D

F_{vert}

B

E

D

B — buoyancy force
D — hydrodynamic drag force

Fig. 6.6 — Aero- and hydrodynamic forces acting on a yacht sailing at an angle of
heel θ.

Although it is clear that a heeling force is thoroughly undesirable it is apparent from Fig. 6.6. that (with the exception of running before the wind) it is impossible to produce a driving force without simultaneously incurring the penalty of a heeling force. Fig. 6.7 summarizes the steady sailing to windward of a yacht and at the same time underlines the words of F. W. Lanchester (1907) who stated that 'the problem of yacht mechanics resolves itself into an aerofoil combination in which the aerofoil acting in the air (the sail) and that acting underwater (the keel) mutually supply each other's reaction'. In other words the mechanics of yachting involves simultaneous consideration of the situation prevailing both above and below the water line.

The yachtsman strives to achieve a situation in which he has a maximum driving force F_D and simultaneously a minimum heeling force F_H since then he will be able to sail at maximum speed with a minimum of drift and heel. Before investigating the mathematics of this requirement we remark that although so far the total aerodynamic force has been resolved into a driving force and a heeling force it is possible to resolve it into a crosswind component L (at right angles to the apparent wind direction) and a drag component D opposing the motion, as shown in Fig. 6.8. It is then easily established that

$$F_D = L \sin\beta - D \cos\beta$$

$$F_H = L \cos\beta + D \sin\beta.$$

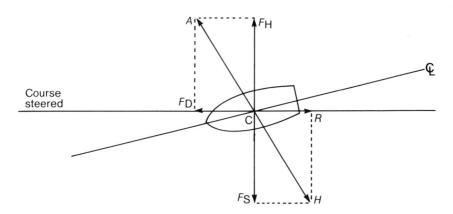

H	—	total hydrodynamic force
F_S	—	hydrodynamic side force
R	—	hydrodynamic resistance force
A	—	total aerodynamic force
F_D	—	driving force
F_H	—	heeling force

Fig. 6.7 – Equilibrium of aero- and hydrodynamic forces in steady sailing.

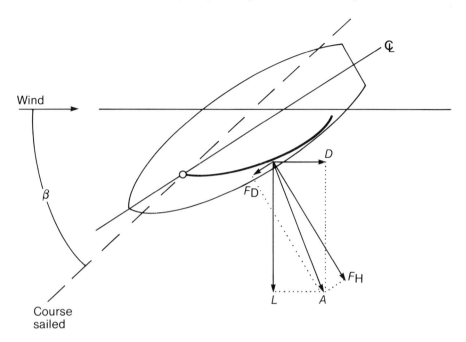

Fig. 6.8 – Alternative resolution of total aerodynamic force into a crosswind force L (at right-angles to the wind), and a drag force D.

These equations imply that the drag force D has the twofold disadvantage of reducing the driving force and increasing the heeling force. The limiting value of β for which sailing to windward is possible occurs when the total aerodynamic force acts in a direction perpendicular to the yacht's course since then there is no driving component in the direction of the course, i.e.

$$L \sin\beta - D \cos\beta = 0$$

so that $\cot\beta = L/D$.

If the drag force was reduced by a small amount δD (see Fig. 6.9) then, for the same crosswind force L, the direction of the total aerodynamic force would be changed from A to A' to produce a non-zero driving component, F_D'. This explains the attention which yachtsmen give to reducing the drag effects of their sails, rigging and hull.

A further complexity is introduced by the fact that the wind speed varies with height above sea level as does the width of the sail, from its maximum at the boom to zero at the mast head. Together these imply that an angle of incidence (the angle between the chord of the sail and the apparent wind direction) of the sail which corresponds to a maximum aerodynamic sail force near the

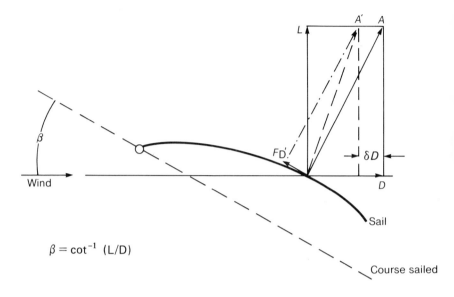

Fig. 6.9 – Diagram to show how a reduction in the drag D corresponding to $\beta = \cot^{-1} (L/D)$ leads to the development of a driving force.

boom could well correspond to a stalled angle of incidence near the head of the sail. Thus as we move up the sail towards the mast head, the angle of incidence changes continuously. This is referred to as the twist of the sail.

The foregoing analysis has so far only included the aerodynamic effects of the wind on the sail. A more rigorous analysis would include the aerodynamic effects produced by the action of the wind on the hull and the rigging. These have been excluded since they can vary considerably from one vessel to another – the sail effects are common to all yachts.

To complete our general analysis of sailing we must examine the hydrodynamic resistance experienced by the hull. Owing to the difficulty and expense of full-scale experiments the design of yacht hulls is usually developed with scale models whose shape can be changed easily and more economically.

We all have some intuitive idea of what is meant by the word streamlined – a fish is streamlined whereas a brick is not! If a streamlined body is introduced into a perfect, or slow, fluid flow then (as shown in Fig. 6.3(a)) the streamlines will close again downstream of the body to form a symmetric pattern with no disturbance. In reality the fluid will encounter some resistance during its flow over the body (or equivalently the body will experience some resistance during its motion through the stationary fluid). Because of this resistance the streamlines will not follow the body contour to the trailing (rear) edge and instead will separate from the surface at some point to form an eddying wake. The pressures on the rear of the body are thus less in magnitude than near the front with the result that a force acts on the body to move it downstream.

Before examining the hydrodynamic resistance in detail we must give some attention to the way in which yacht designers make the transition from their model results to the full-size yacht. To fully understand this we shall need the concepts of Reynolds number and a boundary layer.

6.2 REYNOLDS NUMBER

The forces acting on a full-size vessel are dependent upon the speed and size of the body and the viscosity of the fluid through with it moves. Suppose l is a typical dimension of the full-size vessel (for example the overall length or water-line length) and $l' = \alpha l$ is the corresponding dimension of the model. α is a non-dimensional factor called the scale factor and provides the adjustment between the model coordinates (x', y', z') and the full-size coordinates (x, y, z),

$$x' = \alpha x, \ y' = \alpha y, z' = \alpha z.$$

Similarly if U is a typical velocity in the full size system (for example the speed of the undisturbed flow far away from the vessel) and U' is the corresponding velocity for the model, the velocities would be related by a scale factor β such that

$$U' = \beta U.$$

At the end of the nineteenth century the physicist Reynolds found that if the quantity Ul/ν is kept constant for the two flows then the flow patterns around the model and the full-size vessel are similar. ν denotes the coefficient of kinematic viscosity of the medium and is a combination of its viscous and density properties. The quantity Ul/ν is known as the Reynolds number and is written Re. Reynolds' result is of immense importance to naval architects for it implies that the results of wind tunnel tests on models of sails and hulls can be used to determine the performance of their full-size counterparts. Although the Reynolds number is not precisely defined, since neither U nor l were precisely defined, this does not cause any difficulties, since it is only used to compare similar systems.

6.3 BOUNDARY LAYER

Contrary to its expected stationary behaviour in a perfect fluid flow, the observed downstream movement of an object placed in a fluid flow is explained by the viscous effects of the fluid. In the early twentieth century Prandtl offered the explanation that the flow of a viscous fluid around an object can be divided into two regions. The first is a thin fluid layer, close to the boundary of the object, in which the viscous effects act. He referred to this layer as the boundary layer. The second is the remainder of the flow region in which viscous effects are negligible so that in this second region the flow can be treated as that of a perfect fluid.

It has already been noted that the boundary layer flow may separate from the body before it reaches the rear end. It is explained in Chapter 7 that the wake behind a spinning ball travelling through the air can be made turbulent, and the drag force reduced, if the occurrence of separation can be delayed and that this can be achieved by roughening the surface of the ball. In the case of the airflow around a mast and sail the drag force can be reduced by inducing turbulence in the flow. This can be achieved by, for example, leading a rope down the side of the mast, even a rope of small diameter is sufficient to create turbulence. This idea was used on the 1974 Americas Cup yacht *Courageous* which had a series of small plastic triangles precisely positioned on the front of the mast.

One of the major sources of resistance to the motion of the hull through the water is the skin friction resistance which occurs owing to the presence of the boundary layer. The thicker the boundary layer the greater the mass of water which receives momentum from the hull and hence the greater the energy loss. The skin friction resistance can be calculated from the formula

$$\text{skin friction resistance} = \frac{1}{2} \ C_F \ \rho A v^2$$

where ρ = density of the water, v = velocity of the vessel, A = surface area of wetted part of hull, C_F = skin friction coefficient, dependent upon the nature of the surface of the hull.

The standard of finish of the hull is of obvious importance since any imperfections in the surface finish of the hull will increase the value of C_F and hence increase the magnitude of the skin friction resistance force. The standard of finish of the hull becomes more critical as the design speed of the vessel increases. For non-planing vessels the hull is considered to be hydrodynamically smooth provided that none of the surface imperfections exceeds a thickness of about 6×10^{-5} m. It is therefore worthwile ensuring that the hull is kept free of barnacles and other marine growths! Modern marine paints enable this standard of finish to be easily attained. At low speeds skin friction is the predominant resistance but as the speed of the vessel increases the resistance encountered due to wave making becomes more important. It can account for up to sixty per cent of the total hull resistance. The total energy E lost by a yacht in making waves is proportional to the square of the wave height h and the length of the wave λ i.e.

$$E \propto h^2 \lambda.$$

Froude's law of comparison states that the ratio of wave resistance to displacement is the same for geometrically similar hulls provided that the ratios of speed to the square root of the waterline length are the same. This law therefore enables us to perform experiments on scale models in water tanks and then to predict the behaviour of the full-size vessel from the results. Extensive measurement of both models and full-size yachts has established that the most efficient heavy displacement keel boats achieve a speed:length ratio (defined as $v/\sqrt{L}$)

of 1.4, i.e. a yacht has a maximum speed of 1.4 times the square root of its waterline length. The value of this ratio varies for different types of vessel, for example for naval destroyers the maximum speed attained is approximately $2\sqrt{L}$ while for large passenger liners it is approximately $\sqrt{L}$.

Apart from keel boats there is another type of yacht known as a planing yacht because it travels across the surface of the water rather than through it. Planing is caused by the lift forces generated on the underside of the vessel due to its own speed. Once the ratio of driving force to weight approaches 0.1 the speed is sufficient to drive the vessel up its own bow wave. Planing yachts are typified by a small length to beam ratio (to assist in avoiding earlier bow waves which have travelled aft), shallow draught (to minimize the extent to which the hull must be raised out of the water) and the transition of the hull from a V-shaped forward cross-section to a broad flat-bottomed stern (the V-shape provides for a cleaner bow wave).

6.4 WINGED KEELS

Before concluding the discussion of hulls, mention must be made of the controversy surrounding the keel of the 1983 Americas Cup victor *Australia II*, shown in Fig. 6.10. The controversy was caused by the use of the fins attached to the bottom of the keel. First the Americans protested and wanted the fins banned. Once it had been established that the fins were within the rules there was considerable activity amongst the teams while they fitted fins to their keels in the hope that the performance of their yachts would be improved. Since vast sums of money had been invested in the design of each yacht as a complete entity (sails, rigging, hull and keel) it was not suprising that the outcome of these hastily conducted experiments was to abandon the fins and race with their yachts as originally designed. In a sport like sailing, with so many interdependent variables (performance, sails, rigging, hull, keel) a sudden dramatic change to one of them is likely to have profound effects on many of the others.

We now return to *Australia II* and explain why the fins were fitted in the first place. The flow pattern of the airflow round a wing or equivalently the flow of water round a keel has previously been shown in Fig. 6.1(a). The situation depicted there is idealized due to the fact that the wing is assumed to have infinite span so that the effects of the wing tips can be ignored. In practice the presence of a wing tip (or equivalently the bottom of the keel) has a considerable effect on the flow pattern around that portion near the tip since the crossflow force reduces in magnitude toward the tip. More important within the present context of sailing is the fact that the airflow over and around the wing tip causes the streamline to twist itself up to form a vortex at the tip which is subsequently shed to pass downstream as shown in Fig. 6.10(a). These can be seen quite clearly when a high-speed aircraft makes a sharp turn, the vortex develops while still attached to the wing tip and is then thrown off. These tip

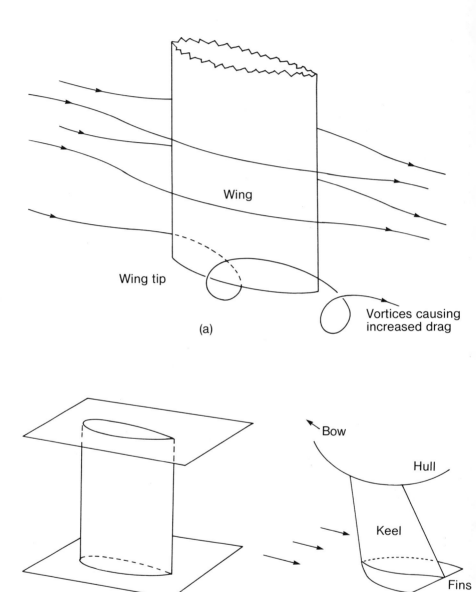

Fig. 6.10 − (a) Tip effects. (b) End plate concept. (c) Keel fins.

vortices alter the flow around the aerofoil section (wing or keel) in such a way that the drag forces can be considerably increased and so reduce the speed of the wing (or keel).

If sufficiently large plates are fitted to the ends of the wing (at right-angles to the plane of the wing) then the flow around the tip is prevented, see Fig. 6.10(b), and the flow over the wing or keel then lacks the tip vortices and is very similar to that shown in Fig. 6.1(a). The use of such end plates is not new; the original patent was taken out in 1897 by F. W. Lanchester. In the case of a yacht, fitting fins at the end of the keel provides one end plate, at the top of the keel the hull is essentially the other end plate as illustrated in Fig. 6.10(c). An additional benefit of the fins is that when the yacht is heeled over, the width of the fins has a vertical component which effectively increases the length of the keel and so increases the hydrodynamic force available to counteract the heeling effects of the sail.

6.5 WINDSURFING

In view of its immense popularity, no chapter on sailing would be complete without a section on windsurfing. Fig. 6.11 shows a sketch of a windsurfer and the forces acting on him. The majority of windsurfers set the boom at shoulder height and perpendicular to the mast with their arms in the same plane as the boom. Let P denote the pull in the arms, W denote the weight of the windsurfer and R denote the resultant reaction between the board and the feet. Since the windsurfer is in equilibrium then resolution of these forces parallel and perpendicular to the horizon gives

$$R \cos \theta - P \cos \phi = 0. \tag{6.1}$$

$$R \sin \theta + P \sin \phi = W. \tag{6.2}$$

It is of some interest to determine P, the pull experienced by the windsurfer's arms. From equations (6.1) and (6.2)

$$P = \frac{W}{\sin \phi + \cos \phi \cdot \tan \theta}. \tag{6.3}$$

While it is obviously a simple matter to determine W by weighing the windsurfer and to measure ϕ from either film or a photograph, the determination of θ (the inclination to the horizontal of the line of action of R) is not so straightforward. In order for the system to remain in equilibrium the line of action of R must pass through the point of intersection of P and W — if it did not then R would have a non-zero moment about the point of intersection of P and W with a consequent soaking for the windsurfer. Therefore we must either find a way of calculating θ or, alternatively, eliminate it from the expression for P. For the body position shown in Fig. 6.11 the centre of mass G of the windsurfer is

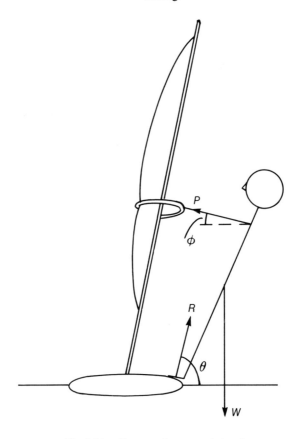

Fig. 6.11 − Forces acting on a windsurfer.

located approximately on a line drawn across the hips. It is then a simple matter to measure the distances d_1 and d_2 from G to the feet and shoulders (considered to be the point of application of P). Referring to Fig. 6.12 we find

$$\tan \theta = \frac{QL'}{FL'} = \frac{QL + LL'}{d_1 \cos \psi}$$

$$= \frac{d_2 \cos \psi \tan \phi + (d_1 + d_2) \sin \psi}{d_1 \cos \psi}$$

i.e.

$$\tan \theta = \frac{d_2}{d_1} \tan \phi + \left(1 + \frac{d_2}{d_1}\right) \tan \psi \tag{6.4}$$

Combination of equations (6.3) and (6.4) then enables us to determine the pull

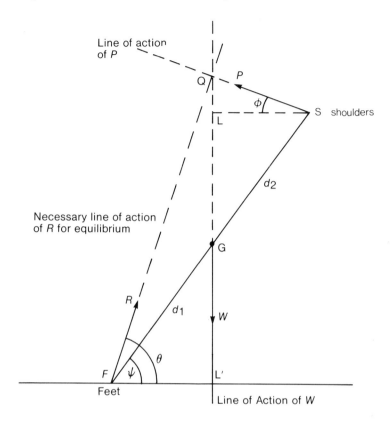

Fig. 6.12 – Diagram to show line of action of R required for equilibrium of windsurfer.

in the arms from a knowledge of the windsurfer's body weight and angles which are easily obtained from photographs or cine film.

For example, photographic analysis shows that reasonable values for the angles and distances involved in equations (6.3) and (6.4) are

$$\psi = 30°, \phi = 45°, d_1 = 1.2 \text{ m and } d_2 = 0.5 \text{ m so that}$$

$$\tan \theta = \frac{0.5}{1.2} \tan 45° + \left(1 + \frac{0.5}{1.2}\right) \tan 30° = 1.2346$$

Thus for a windsurfer weighing 65 kg,

$$P = \frac{65}{\sin 45° + \tan \theta \cdot \cos 45°} = 41.14 \text{ kg,}$$

which is a considerable force to sustain for any length of time.

Consider next the forces acting on the windsurfing board and sail. These are shown in Fig. 6.13(a) and consist of

P,   the pull of the windsurfer on the boom,
M,   the resultant force at the foot of the mast,
A,   the resultant aerodynamic force acting on the sail which acts at the centre of pressure of the board and sail,
W_B, the weight of the boom, mast and sail.

Since the system is in equilibrium then taking moments about the foot of the mast gives

$$P . d_3 + W_B . d_4 \cos \alpha - N . d_5 = 0,$$

where N denotes the component of A which is perpendicular to the mast. Hence

$$N = \frac{d_3}{d_5} P + \frac{d_4}{d_5} \cos \alpha . W_B .$$

Using typical values of $\alpha \stackrel{\sim}{=} 40°, d_3 \stackrel{\sim}{=} 1.4$ m, $d_4 \stackrel{\sim}{=} 1.5$ m, $d_5 \stackrel{\sim}{=} 2.3$ m and $W_B = 9$ kg (a detailed derivation of d_5 is presented in section 6.6 under the heading 'centre of pressure') we find that

$$N = \frac{1.4}{2.3} \times 41.14 + \frac{1.5}{2.3} \times 9 \times \cos 40° = 29.54 \text{ kg.}$$

Finally, consider the forces acting on the board. In this analysis we shall assume that the board is being sailed flat on the water surface and that the windsurfer is standing on the edge of the board as shown in Fig. 6.13(b). Let S denote the hydrodynamic sideforce due to the action of the water on the centreboard acting at the centre of pressure of the keel, which is assumed to be the geometric centre of the rectangular keel, and let H_B denote the buoyancy force acting on the board and windsurfer then

$$X + R_H = S$$

and, taking moments about the foot of the mast

$$R_V . d_7 - S . d_6 = 0.$$

Combining these last two equations gives

$$X = \frac{d_7}{d_6} R_V - R_H \qquad\qquad (6.5)$$

From equation (6.1) $R = P \cos \phi / \cos \theta$
and since $R_V = R \sin \theta$
then $R_V = P \cos \phi . \tan \theta .$
Also $\tan \theta = R_V/R_H$ so $R_H = P \cos \phi$ and

(a)

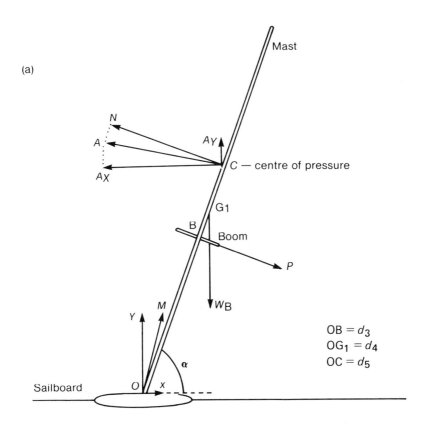

OB $= d_3$
OG$_1$ $= d_4$
OC $= d_5$

(b)

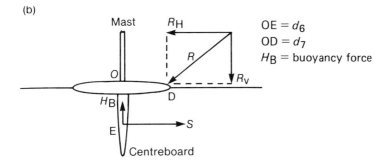

OE $= d_6$
OD $= d_7$
H_B = buoyancy force

Fig. 6.13 — (a) Forces on mast and sail. (b) Forces on sailboard.

equation (6.5) becomes

$$X = P \cos \phi \left(\frac{d_7}{d_6} \tan \theta - 1 \right) ,$$

where $\tan \theta$ is given by equation (6.4). Using typical values of $d_6 = 0.30$ m and $d_7 = 0.35$ m together with the values previously given for ϕ and P results in

$$X = 41.14 \cdot \cos 45° \cdot \left(\frac{0.35}{0.30} \cdot 1.2346 - 1 \right) = 12.81 \text{ kg.}$$

Horizontal resolution of the forces acting on the mast, sail, boom system gives

$$A_X = X + P \sin \alpha$$
$$= 12.81 + 41.14 \sin 40° = 39.25 \text{ kg.}$$

Finally the total aerodynamic force acting on the sail may be resolved either normal to the sail (as N) or alternatively parallel and perpendicular to the horizon (as A_X and A_Y) as shown in Fig. 6.13(a).

It is at once apparent that

$$N = A_X \cos (90° - \alpha) + A_Y \cdot \cos \alpha$$

so that

$$A_Y = \frac{N - A_X \cdot \sin \alpha}{\cos \alpha}$$

$$= \frac{29.54 - 39.25 \sin 40°}{\cos 40°} = 5.63 \text{ kg.}$$

This result means that the airflow over the sail generates a vertical lift force on the system of approximately 5.6 kg.

6.6 CENTRE OF PRESSURE†

Several references have been made in this chapter to a centre of pressure. This point is defined to be the point on a sail (or keel) at which the total aerodynamic (or hydrodynamic) force may be considered to act. For those readers familiar with the techniques of multiple integration the determination of the coordinates of the centre of pressure of the wind effects on the sail of a windsurfing board is now presented. Fig. 6.14(a) shows a typical sailboard. Detail measurements vary from one board to another depending upon the age and ability of the windsurfer. For simplicity the mast is assumed to be vertical and the sail to be of triangular shape. Referred to the axes shown in Fig. 6.14(b) the equations of the edges of the sail are

$$y = -2x + 4.5 \quad \text{and} \quad y = 0.5x.$$

†This section can be omitted if you are not familiar with multiple integration.

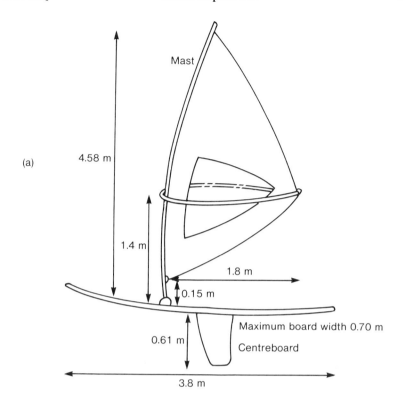

(a)

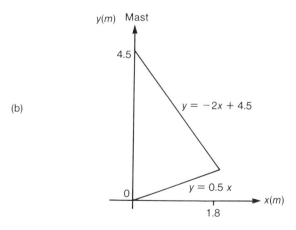

(b)

Fig. 6.14 — Typical sailboard dimensions and simplified sail plan used in centre of pressure calculation.

If w is the weight per unit volume of the air, the thrust on a small element δA at the point (x, y) of the sail is

$$wy \sin \theta \,.\, \delta A \,,$$

where θ is the angle between the plane of the sail and the horizontal and $\delta A = \delta x \, \delta y$, the element of area of the sail. The total thrust on the sail is therefore

$$\iint wy \sin \theta \, dA \,,$$

where the integration takes place over the area of the sail. If the coordinates of the centre of pressure are (x_p, y_p) then taking moments about Ox and Oy gives respectively

$$y_p \,.\, w \sin \theta \iint y \, dA = \iint y \,.\, wy \sin \theta \, dA = w \sin \theta \iint y^2 \, dA$$

and

$$x_p \,.\, w \sin \theta \iint y \, dA = \iint x \,.\, wy \sin \theta \, dA = w \sin \theta \iint xy \, dA$$

so that

$$x_p = \frac{\iint xy \, dA}{\iint y \, dA} \quad \text{and} \quad y_p = \frac{\iint y^2 \, dA}{\iint y \, dA} \quad,$$

$dA = dx \, dy$ and the integrations take place over the area of the sail so that x must range from 0 to 1.8 and for each of these values of x, y must range from $0.5x$ to the value $(-2x + 4.5)$.

We now evaluate each of the integrals involved. First,

$$\iint y \, dA = \int_{x=0}^{1.8} \int_{y=0.5x}^{-2x+4.5} y \, dy \, dx \ .$$

Since the limits of integration for y involve the variable x, then the y integration must be performed first to give

$$\int_{x=0}^{1.8} \left[\frac{y^2}{2} \right]_{0.5x}^{-2x+4.5} dx$$

$$= \frac{1}{2} \int_0^{1.8} ((-2x + 4.5)^2 - 0.25x^2) \, dx$$

$$= \frac{1}{2} \left[-\frac{1}{6} (-2x + 4.5)^3 - \frac{0.25}{3} x^3 \right]_0^{1.8} = 7.29 \ .$$

Next consider

$$\iint y^2 \, dA = \int_{x=0}^{1.8} \int_{y=0.5x}^{-2x+4.5} y^2 \, dy \, dx$$

$$= \int_0^{1.8} \left[\frac{y^3}{3}\right]_{0.5x}^{-2x+4.5} dx$$

$$= \frac{1}{3} \int_0^{1.8} ((-2x+4.5)^3 - 0.125x^3) \, dx$$

$$= \frac{1}{3} \left[-\frac{1}{8}(-2x+4.5)^4 - \frac{0.125}{4}x^4\right]_0^{1.8} = 16.95 \; .$$

Finally

$$\iint xy \, dA = \int_{x=0}^{1.8} \int_{y=0.5x}^{-2x+4.5} xy \, dy \, dx$$

$$= \int_{x=0}^{1.8} x \left[\frac{y^2}{2}\right]_{0.5x}^{-2x+4.5} dx$$

$$= \frac{1}{2} \int_0^{1.8} (x(-2x+4.5)^2 - 0.25x^3) \, dx.$$

In view of the high powers of x now involved, the first integral is most readily evaluated using integration by parts to give

$$\frac{1}{2} \left\{ \left[\frac{x(-2x+4.5)}{-6}\right]_0^{1.8} + \frac{1}{6} \int_0^{1.8} (-2x+4.5)^3 \, dx - \frac{0.25}{4}\left[x^4\right]_0^{1.8} \right\}$$

$$= \frac{1}{2} \left\{ -\frac{1.8 \times 0.9^3}{6} - \frac{1}{48}\left[(-2x+4.5)^4\right]_0^{1.8} - \frac{0.25 \times 1.8^4}{4} \right\}$$

$$= 3.83.$$

Thus $x_p = 3.83/7.29 \doteq 0.5$ and $y_p = 16.95/7.29 \doteq 2.3$, which was the value used earlier for d_s.

6.7 PUMPING

Sometimes one sees a helmsman alternately sheet the sail in abruptly thereby suddenly increasing the angle of incidence and then subsequently ease it gradually away to leeward. The action is repeated to produce a kind of pumping action.

To an observer it appears that the helmsman is aiding the propulsion of the boat with this muscular action in contravention of the sailing regulation which states that no means of propulsion is allowed other than the natural action of the wind on the sails. The phenomenon can be explained with reference to Fig. 6.15 which shows the variation of the driving force with the angle of incidence, of the chord of the sail, to the wind.

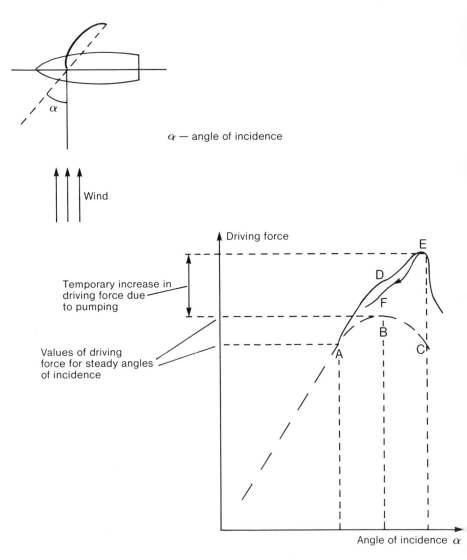

Fig. 6.15 – Diagram to explain the temporary increase in propulsive force due to pumping.

As the angle of incidence is gradually increased the dotted curve shows how the driving force builds up to a maximum value and then decreases again. However, if the angle of incidence is suddenly increased to a value which for steady flow would correspond to some separated flow over the sail, the flow continues to adhere smoothly to the sail with a corresponding increase in the driving force of up to forty-five per cent, as shown by the solid curve in Fig. 6.15.

If this larger angle of incidence is maintained, then eventually separation will occur and the driving force will diminish, to C. If instead the sail is eased gradually it is possible to return to the situation represented by the point A, via the path EFA.

The pumping action used to decrease and increase the angle of incidence can then be repeated to obtain the benefit of further short-term increases in the driving force. The pumping action is therefore within the rules since its effects are due to action of the wind on the sails.

6.8 RELATIVE VELOCITY

Owing to the motion of the yacht itself, the wind speed and direction experienced by the crew are very different from the true wind speed and direction. The explanation of this observation requires the concept of relative velocity which may be defined as

Relative velocity of A with respect to an observer B = $\mathbf{V}_A - \mathbf{V}_B$,

where $\mathbf{V}_A$ = velocity of A relative to some fixed axes and $\mathbf{V}_B$ = velocity of observer B relative to the same fixed axes.

In order to show the effect that the motion of the observer has on the relative, or apparent, wind velocity suppose that a crewman on a yacht which is sailing due North at eight knots records the wind speed and direction as ten knots blowing from the North East. If a set of Cartesian axes Oxy with their associated unit vectors $\mathbf{i}$ and $\mathbf{j}$ is introduced so that the x axis points East and the y axis points North then from Fig. 6.16(a) we see that the true velocity of the yacht, $\mathbf{V}_y = 8\mathbf{j}$ and the relative velocity of the wind with respect to the yacht

$$= -10 \cos 45° \, \mathbf{i} - 10 \sin 45° \, \mathbf{j}$$

$$= -7.071\mathbf{i} - 7.071\mathbf{j}.$$

If $\mathbf{V}_w$ denotes the true velocity of the wind then, using the equation given at the beginning of this section

$$-7.071\mathbf{i} - 7.071\mathbf{j} = \mathbf{V}_w - 8\mathbf{j}$$

so

$$\mathbf{V}_w = -7.071\mathbf{i} + 0.929\mathbf{j} \, .$$

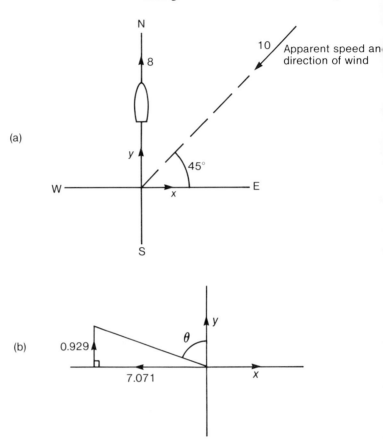

Fig. 6.16 – Apparent and real wind components.

The magnitude of the true velocity of the wind is thus

$$\sqrt{((-7.071)^2 + 0.929^2)} = 7.13 \text{ knots},$$

and the true direction of the wind may be obtained from the velocity triangle shown in Fig. 6.16(b) as $N\theta°W$ where

$$\theta = \text{arc tan} (7.071/0.929) = 82°31'.$$

The true wind velocity is thus 7.13 knots blowing in the direction N 82° 31′ W which is vastly different from the apparent wind velocity as observed by the crewman.

It is not only the course and speed of the wind which is affected in the manner just described but those of any moving object which is viewed by a moving observer.

For example, suppose yachtsman A is sailing North West at six knots and wishes to determine the true course and speed of a hovercraft which to him appears to be travelling due East at twenty knots. Referred to the coordinate axes introduced in the previous example we may write

$$\text{true velocity of yachtsman, } \mathbf{V_A} = -6 \cos 45° \, \mathbf{i} + 6 \sin 45° \, \mathbf{j}$$

$$= -4.243 \, \mathbf{i} + 4.243 \, \mathbf{j} \; ,$$

relative velocity of the hovercraft with respect to the yacht $= 20\mathbf{i}$.

If $\mathbf{V_H}$ denotes the true velocity of the hovercraft then

$$20\mathbf{i} = \mathbf{V_H} - (-4.243\mathbf{i} + 4.243\mathbf{j})$$

so

$$\mathbf{V_H} = 15.757\mathbf{i} + 4.243\mathbf{j}.$$

The magnitude of the true velocity of the hovercraft is then

$$\sqrt{(15.757^2 + 4.243^2)} = 16.32 \text{ knots}$$

and its true course is $N\theta° \, E$ where

$$\theta = \text{arc tan}(15.757/4.243) = 74°56' \; .$$

The last two examples show that in sailing, as with many other sports, it is essential to distinguish between true courses and speeds (measured with respect to some fixed origin) and relative, or apparent, courses and speeds (measured with respect to a moving origin, usually the observer).

7

Ball Games

7.1 THE DIFFERENT POSSIBLE LEVELS OF ANALYSIS OF BALL GAMES

There are many games such as soccer and basketball which are played with a spherical ball. Other sports such as cricket use an almost spherical ball (the deviation from a spherical shape is caused by the seam of the ball), while games like rugby and American football use a ball of ellipsoidal shape.

There are several levels of sophistication of mathematical treatment which can be applied to the analysis of ball games. First, the three levels are defined and then each is considered separately.

(1) The ball is treated as a rigid sphere assumed to be moving in a vacuum. This model forms the basis for the snooker and bat–ball collision problems which are so popular with examiners!

(2) The ball is still treated as a rigid sphere but allowance is made for the effects of both the medium through which the ball moves and any spin which is imparted to the ball. This model provides the basis for explaining, for example, the variations from a parabola exhibited by the ball's trajectory and the phenomenon of a sliced shot in golf or tennis.

(3) The final stage involves the consideration of the aerodynamic phenomenon of turbulence in the airflow around the ball. Perhaps contrary to one's expectations, the turbulence can be used to advantage in certain games, for example golf. Creating turbulence is the reason for the dimpled surface of a golf ball.

7.2 ELEMENTARY COLLISION THEORY

There is a large group of ball games which involve the impact of one body with another and in which the participants success depends upon their ability to predict the motion of the ball after impact. For example players need to be able to predict the motion of a snooker ball after impact with another ball or the cushion, or a squash ball after impact with a wall, or a cricket ball or baseball after impact with a bat. If they cannot do this then they may position themselves incorrectly and thus find it difficult or impossible to play a successful shot.

Since impacts and their consequences are so important in sport we investigate the factors which determine the outcome of an impact between two bodies.

Elasticity
When a ball is hit by another ball or a bat (or equivalently when a ball hits a fixed surface) both the ball and the bat deform slightly. As each body subsequently regains its original shape the ball rebounds from the bat. This ability to regain its original shape is known as the elasticity of the material.

Coefficient of Restitution
The tendency of a body to return to its original shape after impact varies from one body to another depending upon the material. It is obviously important to quantify this phenomenon in order to be able to predict the outcome of an impact. Following experimental work in this field, Sir Isaac Newton was able to postulate his law of impact:

If two bodies move towards each other and collide the difference between their velocities along the line of centres immediately after impact is proportional to the difference between their velocities measured along the line of centres immediately before impact. The constant of proportionality is denoted by $-e$, where e is called the coefficient of restitution.

$$v_1 - v_2 = -e\,(u_1 - u_2),\qquad (7.1)$$

see Fig. 7.1.

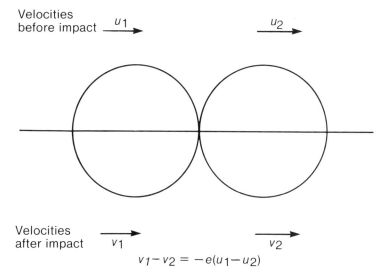

Velocities before impact $\underrightarrow{u_1}$ $\underrightarrow{u_2}$

Velocities after impact $\;\;v_1\;\; \qquad v_2$

$$v_1 - v_2 = -e(u_1 - u_2)$$

Fig. 7.1 – Diagram to illustrate Newton's law of impact.

The value of the coefficient of restitution depends upon the material of both the objects which collide together. To illustrate this, consider the simple experiment illustrated in Fig. 7.2 of dropping a ball of mass m and radius a onto the floor (a fixed surface). If suffix 1 refers to the ball and suffix 2 refers to the floor then

$$u_2 = v_2 = 0$$

and Newton's law of impact reduces to

$$-e = \frac{v_1}{u_1} .$$ (7.2)

u_1 and v_1, the ball velocities immediately before and after impact respectively, can be found by applying the principle of conservation of energy.

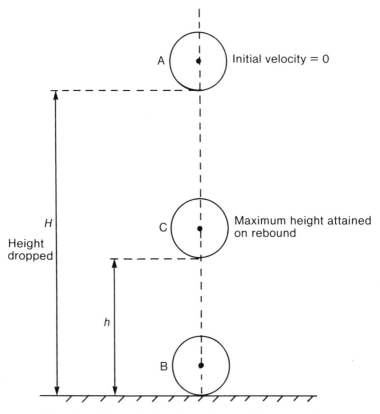

Velocity at B just before impact = u_1 (downwards)
Velocity at B just after impact = v_1 (upwards)

Fig. 7.2 – Experiment to determine coefficient of restitution between ball and floor. Velocity at B just before impact = u_1 (downwards). Velocity at B just after impact = v_1 (upwards).

Neglecting air resistance effects and choosing the level of zero potential energy as the floor, the principle of conservation of energy gives just before impact

$$\text{Total energy at A} \quad = \quad \text{Total energy at B}$$
$$\frac{1}{2} m \times 0^2 + mg(H + a) \quad = \quad \frac{1}{2} mu_1^2 + mga,$$

whence $\qquad u_1 \quad = \quad \sqrt{(2gH)}.$

Similarly just after impact,

$$\text{Total energy at B} \quad = \quad \text{Total energy at C}$$
$$\frac{1}{2} mv_1^2 + mga \quad = \quad \frac{1}{2} m \times 0^2 + mg(h + a)$$
$$v_1 \quad = \quad -\sqrt{(2gh)}.$$

Why do we take the negative square root?

Equation (7.2) then gives the coefficient of restitution as

$$e = \sqrt{\left(\frac{h}{H}\right)} . \tag{7.3}$$

This result enables us to design a very simple experiment to show the variation in the value of e for balls made of different materials. Simply drop a ball from a known height and measure the height to which it rebounds. Equation (7.3) can then be used to determine the coefficient of restitution. Table 7.1 shows the results obtained by the author when different balls were dropped onto a tiled concrete floor. You could conduct a similar experiment using one particular ball and varying the material of the floor in order to investigate how this affects e.

Table 7.1

Coefficient of restitution for balls dropped from a height of 2 m onto a tiled concrete floor.

Ball	Rebound height (h m)	Coefficient of restitution e
Basketball	1.12	0.75
Soccer	1.13	0.75
Tennis (new)	0.90	0.67
Cricket (new)	0.21	0.32

The coefficient of restitution is also affected by the temperature of the ball. For example, prior to a game of squash it is not only the players who need to warm up; the ball too must be warmed up. This is achieved by 'knocking up' with the match ball, the energy lost in the impacts being sufficient to warm the ball. The effect of changes in temperature on the coefficient of restitution can also be investigated by the simple bounce experiment described above. You will need a set of the same type of ball. Put some in a freezer, keep some at room temperature and warm the rest in an oven. Then drop each ball from the same height, measure the rebound height and hence calculate e. You should find that the value of e increases as the temperature of the ball increases; squash and basketball players say the ball becomes more 'lively'.

The actual impacts between bodies are divided into two categories depending upon their motions immediately prior to impact. If both bodies are moving along the normal to the contact surface, the impact is called a direct impact. The striking of a cue ball with a cue is an example of a direct impact. In sport, it is more usual for the bodies not to collide 'head-on' and these collisions are known as oblique impacts. A bounce pass in basketball is an example of an oblique impact. Prior to impact with the ground the ball is travelling at an acute angle to the ground. Most of the strokes played in racket games involve oblique impacts so that the impact not only returns the ball in the direction from which it came but also causes it to move away from the opponent's position thereby gaining an advantage for the striker.

Fig. 7.3(a) shows the oblique impact of a ball bouncing against a fixed wall. The velocity of the ball immediately prior to the instant of contact is denoted by u in the direction shown on the diagram. Since both the ball and the wall are assumed to be smooth there is no force horizontally on the ball. Its horizontal motion is therefore unchanged and so

$$v \sin \phi = u \sin \theta .$$

The vertical component of velocity undergoes major changes. The impact reverses its direction and the elasticity of the ball and the wall changes the magnitude of this component in accordance with Newton's law of impact

$$v \cos \phi - 0 = -e(-u \cos \theta - 0)$$

so that

$$v \cos \phi = e\, u \cos \theta .$$

Since $e < 1$ the vertical component of the ball's velocity after impact is less than it was prior to impact.

Using a terminology borrowed from optics, the angle which the ball's velocity makes with the perpendicular to the surface is called the angle of incidence

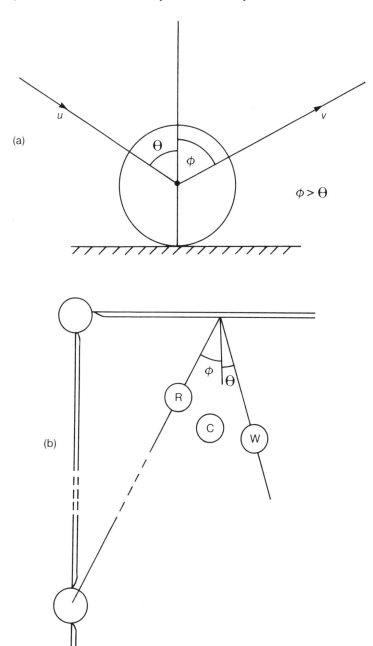

Fig. 7.3 – (a) Oblique impact – angles of incidence (θ) and reflection (ϕ). (b) Oblique impact in snooker.

(prior to impact) and the angle of reflection (after impact). From the above two equations

$$\tan \phi = \frac{1}{e} \tan \theta \tag{7.4}$$

so that, since $e < 1$,

$$\phi = \text{arc} \tan \left(\frac{1}{e} \tan \theta \right) > \theta,$$

i.e. the angle of reflection is greater than the angle of incidence. This result is only true for oblique impacts in which one object is fixed throughout and frictional effects are ignored. A striking example (no pun intended) of the application of the above result occurs in the snooker shot shown in Fig. 7.3(b) in which the cue ball W must strike the red ball R without first touching the coloured ball C. Knowing the angle ϕ required to ultimately 'pot' the red ball, equation (7.4) can be used to determine the appropriate angle of incidence θ. The player can then execute an oblique impact at a point on the cushion somewhere behind the coloured ball which remains untouched.

The final type of impact which we discuss in this section is an oblique impact between two moving bodies such as the impact between a cricket bat or baseball bat and a ball. Fig. 7.4(a) shows a typical bat and ball oblique impact at the instant before impact while Fig. 7.4(b) shows the velocity components of the bat and ball immediately before and after impact.

Application of Newton's law of impact along the line of centres (PO) gives

$$W - w = -e(-U \cos \alpha - u) \tag{7.5}$$

where e represents the coefficient of restitution for a ball–bat impact. If m_1 denotes the mass of the bat and m_2 the mass of the ball then application of the principle of conservation of momentum along the line of centres gives

$$m_1 u + m_2 \times (-U \cos \alpha) = m_1 w + m_2 W. \tag{7.6}$$

The quantities of most interest in such an impact are the speed and direction of the ball after it has been hit. We thus solve equations (7.5) and (7.6) for W. This is easily performed by eliminating w between equations (7.5) and (7.6) to give

$$W = \frac{m_1 u (1 + e) + U \cos \alpha (m_1 e - m_2)}{m_1 + m_2}.$$

Since there is no force acting at right angles to the line PO at impact then there is no change in the motion in this direction and hence

$$V = U \sin \alpha. \tag{7.7}$$

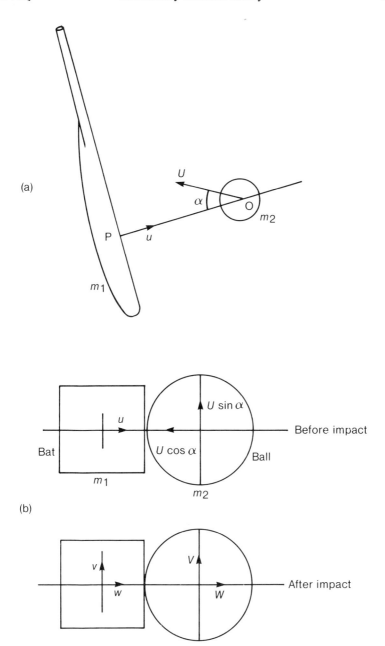

Fig. 7.4 – (a) Bat and ball immediately before impact. (b) Velocity components of bat and ball before and after impact.

The magnitude of the velocity of the ball after impact with the bat is therefore given by

$$\sqrt{(W^2 + U^2 \sin^2 \alpha)},$$

and the direction of motion after impact is inclined at an angle ϕ to the normal to the bat given by

$$\phi = \text{arc tan} \left(\frac{U \sin \alpha}{W} \right). \tag{7.8}$$

Once the value of e has been obtained using the bounce experiment to drop the ball onto a horizontal bat, equations (7.7) and (7.8) can then be used to determine the motion of the ball immediately after impact. For example the following cricket data

mass of bat (m_1)	$= 1.02$ kg
mass of ball (m_2)	$= 0.156$ kg
velocity of ball before impact (U)	$= 30$ ms^{-1}
velocity of bat before impact (u)	$= 12$ ms^{-1}
typical value of e	$= 0.3$
typical value of α	$= 30°$

gives the velocity of the ball after impact as 22.56 ms^{-1} in a direction $41.7°$ to the normal to the bat.

You may like to repeat the calculations using the following baseball data

mass of bat (m_1)	$= 1.02$ kg
mass of ball (m_2)	$= 0.15$ kg
velocity of ball before impact (U)	$= 36$ ms^{-1}
velocity of bat before impact (u)	$= 15$ ms^{-1}
typical value of e	$= 0.5$
typical value of α	$= 30°$.

Alternatively you could keep all the variables fixed except one, perhaps the velocity of the bat before impact, and investigate the effect on the ball's velocity after impact of variations in the velocity of the bat.

Your results should indicate that to achieve a high ball velocity after impact, and hence a long-range shot, you should use a heavy bat, hit a ball moving at high velocity and swing the bat vigorously so that it has a high velocity at impact.

7.3 THE EFFECTS OF SKIDDING AND SPINNING

Our second level of mathematical analysis of ball games acknowledges the contribution of the skidding and spinning which the ball experiences. Observation of a billiards or snooker match shows that once the cue ball has been hit it usually spins and skids for some time before commencing its pure rolling motion. One of the most remarkable illustrations of this is the snooker shot in which the cue ball collides directly with a stationary object ball (possibly situated at the other end of the table) after which the cue ball returns back to or beyond its original position. The laws of particle dynamics used in the analysis of oblique impacts do not predict such behaviour so one is led to question how such a result is achieved. The answer is provided by the fact that the cue ball is hit off-centre — in fact the cue hits the ball at a point below the level of the ball's centre of mass. The resulting moment of this impulsive blow about the centre of the ball is anticlockwise so that the cue ball moves off with an anticlockwise skidding motion (see Fig. 7.5). Owing to the friction between the ball and the

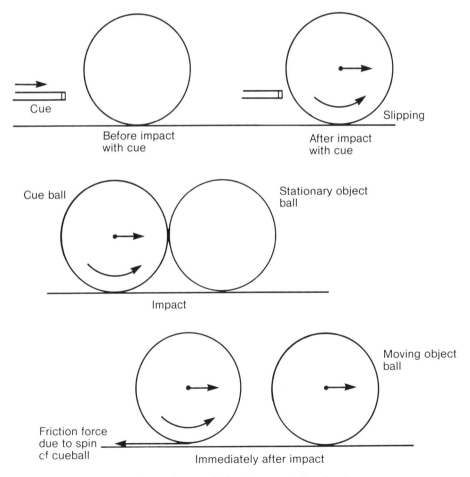

Fig. 7.5 — Off-centre impact between ball and cue results in a skidding motion of the ball.

table the skidding will eventually cease at which time the ball will commence to roll. Before this happens the cue ball collides with its stationary target, called the object ball. In this collision the speed of the cue ball is reduced, but it is still spinning and the frictional force acting on it acts from right to left (see Fig. 7.5). The cue ball, still spinning, therefore begins to move to the left. Eventually the frictional effects between the cue ball and the table reduce the spin to zero at which time the cue ball begins to roll.

The effect of the initial off-centre blow and the subsequent collision can therefore enable the player to return the cue ball back to or beyond its original position should he wish. It is thus apparent that the deliberate introduction of spin can be extremely beneficial. It is of interest to determine the duration of the skidding phase of the cue ball's motion. To do this consider the motion of a ball across a horizontal surface caused by the action of a horizontal blow directed towards the centre of the ball, as shown in Fig. 7.6. No initial rotation is imparted to the ball because the blow is directed towards the centre of the ball. The initial motion of the ball is to skid from left to right over the surface with an initial velocity v_0. Once the ball is moving a frictional force F begins to act from right to left between the ball and the horizontal surface of amount $F = \mu mg$ where m denotes the mass of the ball and μ denotes the coefficient of sliding friction

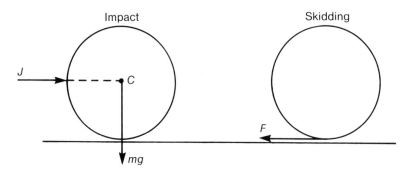

Fig. 7.6 – Duration of the skidding phase.

between the ball and the table. The effect of the friction force is twofold. First it produces a linear deceleration of the ball and secondly, owing to its clockwise moment about the centre of the ball it produces a clockwise angular acceleration of the ball. Using Newton's second law of motion the linear deceleration is given by $F/m = \mu g$ while its angular acceleration is given by aF/I where a is the radius of the ball and I is the moment of inertia of the solid ball about a diameter. Since $I = 2ma^2/5$, the angular acceleration of the ball is $5\mu g/2a$. At time t after impact the velocity of the ball is given by

$$v = v_0 - \mu gt.$$

The angular acceleration of the ball can be integrated once with respect to time to give w the angular velocity of the ball as

$$w = \frac{5\mu g}{2a} \, t + \text{constant.}$$

The value of the arbitrary constant of integration may be determined from the initial condition that at time $t = 0$ the ball has zero angular acceleration. This gives the value of the constant of integration as zero so that w the angular velocity of the ball at time t after impact is

$$w = \frac{5\mu g}{2a} \, t.$$

The skidding phase will cease once the linear velocity has reduced and the angular velocity has increased to such an extent that rolling occurs. Rolling begins when

$$v = aw$$

$$v_0 - \mu g t = \frac{5\mu g}{2} \, t$$

so

$$t = \frac{2v_0}{7\mu g} \quad .$$

Experiments have shown that for snooker and billiards typical values of μ and v_0 are 0.2 and 3 ms^{-1} respectively so that the skidding phase lasts for approximately 0.4 s. The distance travelled (s m) during the skidding phase can be determined from

$$s = v_0 \cdot \frac{2v_0}{7\mu g} - \frac{1}{2} \, \mu g \cdot \left(\frac{2v_0}{7\mu g}\right)^2 = \frac{12v_0^2}{49\mu g} \quad .$$

(This equation can be used since the linear deceleration of the ball is constant.)

For the above values, the length of the skidding phase is 1.1 m. Notice that s depends on the square of v_0 so that even a small change in v_0 will have a marked effect on the length of the skidding phase.

Of course snooker and billiards players sometimes wish to impart a pure rolling motion without skidding to the ball from the moment of impact and we shall return to this problem later in the chapter.

7.4 THE EFFECT OF THE MEDIUM THROUGH WHICH THE BALL MOVES

So far the nature of the medium through which the ball is moving has been ignored. In fact the medium through which the ball moves can have a profound effect upon its behaviour. In the absence of spin the resistance effects of the medium (usually air) serve only to reduce the velocity of the ball and hence alter its trajectory. The combination of spin and air resistance effects can, depending upon the orientation of the axis about which the ball is spinning, cause the ball to move off its intended path to left or right or up or down. This phenomenon is well known to sportsmen who exploit it to the full in, for example, tennis, table tennis, baseball and golf. The spin is imparted deliberately in order to produce certain desired effects. In tennis it is used to cause the ball to drop unexpectedly quickly into the opponent's court. On the other hand a sliced shot on the golf course is an example of unwanted spin since it causes the ball to veer off the intended course to one side. It should be mentioned that spin is also used constructively on the golf course − the effect of bottomspin (see Fig. 7.7) is to increase the range of the drive from the tee to the green.

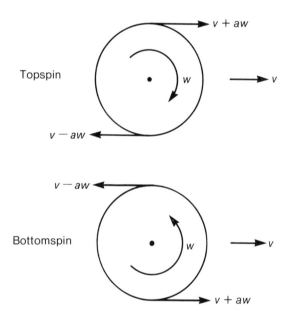

Fig. 7.7 − Topspin and bottomspin − ball of radius a moving left to right with velocity v and spinning about a horizontal axis with angular velocity w.

The terms topspin and bottomspin are used to describe the sense of the rotation of the ball. Topspin refers to the case in which the top of the ball is moving forwards relative to the centre, while bottomspin describes the case in which the bottom of the ball is moving forward relative to the centre.

Before we examine the consequences of spin in a variety of ball games we must discuss more fully how the ball acquires the spin. The explanation has already been touched upon in the discussion of skidding snooker balls: the spin is caused by the off-centre impact between the ball and another object. To illustrate the idea further, consider the impact between a golf club and a golf ball. Even though the ball might be hit by the centre of the club face, some spin about a horizontal diameter will be imparted to the ball unless the centre of mass of the clubhead is behind the centre of the club face. In Fig. 7.8(b) the centre of mass G of the clubhead is below the level of the centre of the ball with the result that the impact will cause the bottom of the ball to move faster than the centre resulting in bottomspin. If G was above the level of C, topspin would be imparted

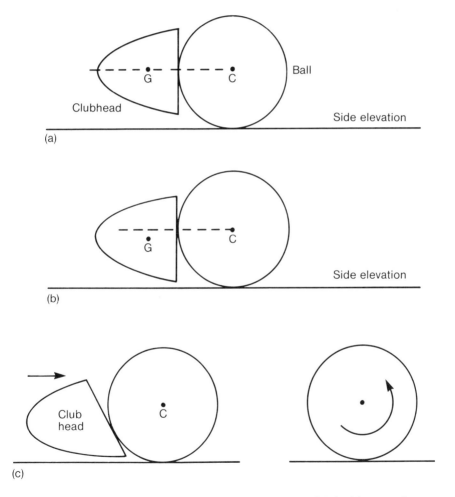

Fig. 7.8 – (a) Clubface perpendicular to direction of travel of club with centre of mass of clubhead behind centre of face – no spin. (b) Centre of mass of clubhead below common normal at impact causing ball to spin. (c) Backspin imparted by a lofted club (side elevation).

to the ball. All clubs are termed lofted as they have the face inclined at an angle to the vertical. The effect of this is that at impact with the ball when the clubhead is travelling horizontally the ball is hit below its centre of mass and thus receives some bottomspin (see Fig. 7.8(c)). Clubs with faces at different inclinations are used to provide varying amounts of bottomspin. The effect of bottomspin is to generate a lift force (see below), a certain amount of which can increase the range of the shot. The more bottomspin the ball is given the higher it can be lofted into the air compared with its trajectory if no spin is imparted to it.

Even if the golfer realizes as he swings the club that his stroke will impart spin to the ball which will result in a sliced shot it is still too late for him to correct the shot during impact. The impact time is of the order of 0.5 ms which is less than the time taken for the effect of the impact to travel up the shaft of the club to the hands and for the resulting sensation to be relayed to the brain. Once the mistake is realized it is too late, the ball has left the clubface!

The effect of the spin on the motion of the ball through the air, now considered to be a viscous medium, is to generate a force perpendicular to the direction of motion. This force, called the Magnus force, can be advantageous or detrimental to the motion depending upon its direction. The origin of the force is as follows. Fig. 7.9(a) shows the motion of a slow-moving viscous medium past a stationary spherical obstacle (or equivalently the passage of a moving sphere through a stationary viscous medium). If the sphere is allowed to spin about an axis perpendicular to the page in the sense shown in Fig. 7.9(b) then because of the viscous effects the sphere will drag the streamlines round with it over the top of the sphere. Consequently the streamlines will be closer together at the top of the sphere than at the bottom so that the pressure on the top of the sphere is less than that below it (for further detail see the reference to Bernoulli's theorem in Chapter 6). As a result the sphere experiences a transverse force in the direction shown in Fig. 7.9(b). If the direction of spin is reversed the Magnus force will act in the opposite direction.

The Magnus force is a maximum if the axis of spin and the direction of the flow are at right angles. If this angle is less than a right angle then the Magnus force is reduced until it reaches zero value if the two axes coincide.

Depending upon the orientation of the axis of spin of the sphere, the effect of the Magnus force is to cause the sphere to swerve off to the left or right, or in the vertical plane to rise or fall.

We now consider the effect of the Magnus force on the ball in a variety of sports.

(i) Baseball

Baseball pitchers have developed throwing techniques which impart a very high rate of spin to the ball (up to twenty-seven revolutions per second have been recorded) which causes a horizontal swerve, over the prescribed pitcher to batter distance, of approximately 0.4 m. Since the time of flight

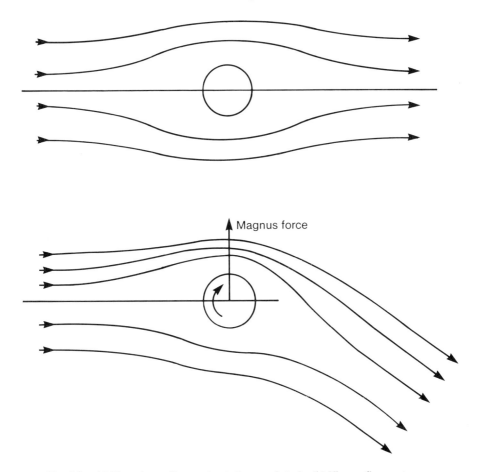

Fig. 7.9 – (a) Slow viscous flow past a stationary obstacle. (b) Viscous flow past a spinning obstacle showing direction of transverse force.

of the ball is quite short the batter does not have very long to adapt his stroke to compensate for the swerve and is thus disadvantaged by this Magnus force effect.

(ii) Tennis and table tennis

In these sports, the ball is often hit when the racket or bat is moving upwards across the ball as shown in Fig. 7.10. The resulting topspin imparted to the ball produces a Magnus force which acts vertically downwards. This causes the ball to drop more quickly into the opponent's court than it would do if no spin effects were introduced. The opponent thus has less time in which to decide upon a strategy for the return stroke.

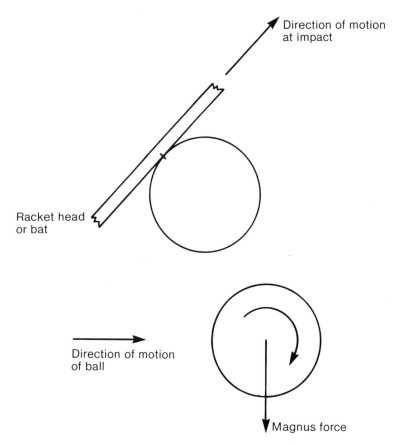

Fig. 7.10 – Oblique impact between racket and ball to impart topspin to ball (side elevation).

(iii) Golf

All golf clubs are designed to impart a certain amount of bottomspin to the ball. If they imparted topspin, this would cause the ball to dive prematurely to the ground. The effect of the bottomspin, about a horizontal axis through the centre of the ball, is to produce a Magnus force which acts vertically upwards thus increasing the time of flight of the shot.

On the other hand if the ball is hit off-centre when viewed horizontally then spin will be generated about a vertical axis of the ball. The resulting Magnus force will then act horizontally to the left or right, depending on the sense of the spin, and cause the ball to swerve off to left or right. Such strokes are said to be hooked or sliced – they are the golfer's nightmare! The Magnus effect can thus be either the golfer's ally or enemy depending upon the axis about which the spin is generated.

(iv) Soccer

The Magnus effect is used to advantage by soccer players who 'bend' the path of a free kick to produce the so called 'banana shot'. Fig. 7.11(a) shows the plan view of an off-centre impact between a soccer ball and a boot. The resulting anticlockwise spin shown in the plan view gives rise to a transverse force which acts to the left as viewed by the player. If the player directs his free kick to the right of the defensive wall (see Fig. 7.11(b)) the effect of the Magnus force will be to bend the ball's path to the left, as seen by the player, once the ball has passed the defensive wall. The resulting path is shown in Fig. 7.11(c) where it can be seen that the goalkeeper's job is made more difficult by the swerve in the path.

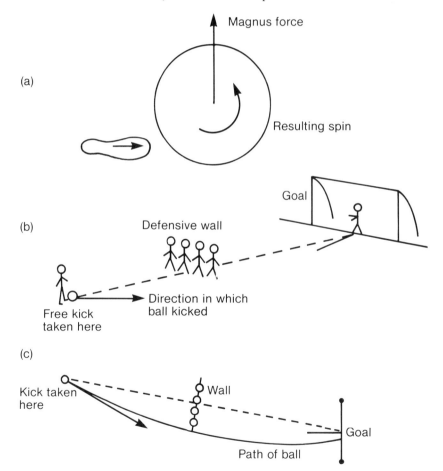

Fig. 7.11 — (a) Impact between soccer ball and foot showing resulting spin and Magnus force (plan view). (b) Soccer freekick. (c) Plan view of freekick showing 'banana' path of ball.

(v) Cricket

Consider a right-handed batsman receiving straight deliveries down the wicket from a bowler. A good bowler will occasionally vary his delivery in an attempt to outwit the batsman. If he spins the ball anticlockwise about a vertical axis viewed from above, the Magnus force will act to the left, as viewed by the bowler, and cause the ball to drift away from the right-handed batsman. The batsman who has become accustomed to receiving straight deliveries from the bowler may find this sudden change of delivery most unsettling!

It was mentioned earlier that occasionally a snooker or billiards player might wish to impart a pure rolling motion to the ball, without skidding, from the moment of impact. To achieve this, the ball must be hit in such a way that the spin imparted to the ball is just sufficient to match the initial translational velocity of the ball. To understand how this is accomplished requires the concept of a centre of percussion which is most easily illustrated with reference to cricket or baseball. Sometimes when the ball is struck, no jaring is felt at the hands. Fig. 7.12(a) shows a rod AB, representing the bat, pivoted at the hands A which receives an impulsive blow J at the point P. Generally an impulsive reaction is induced at A, although it is possible to determine a position for P such that no impulsive reaction is felt at A. This position of P is called the centre of percussion and can be located as follows.

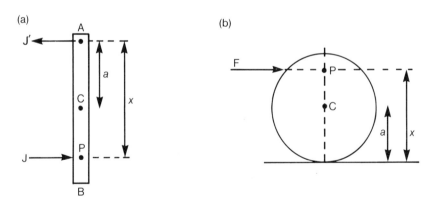

Fig. 7.12 — Diagram to illustrate centre of percussion calculation for cue-ball impact.

Let m denote the mass of the rod and let I be its moment of inertia about the axis of rotation through A perpendicular to the rod. Taking moments about A gives

$$Iw = Jx,$$

where w denotes the change in angular velocity of the rod. Since the rod is assumed to be at rest initially, the initial velocity of the centre of mass G is aw so that if J' denotes the impulsive reaction at A

$$J - J' = maw.$$

When $J' = 0$, elimination of J between the above two equations gives

$$x = I/ma,$$

where x now represents the distance of the centre of percussion of the rod from its axis of rotation.

If this result is applied to the ball shown in Fig. 7.12(b) then we shall obtain the value of x such that a horizontal blow applied to the ball at this height above the table causes no impulsive reaction at the contact point A, i.e. the ball rolls without skidding from the beginning of its motion.

For a solid sphere of mass m and radius a the moment of inertia about a diameter is $2ma^2/5$. Using the parallel axes theorem, its moment of inertia about a horizontal axis through the point of contact with the ground is thus

$$I = \frac{2ma^2}{5} + ma^2 = \frac{7ma^2}{5} .$$

The centre of percussion of the ball is then at a height $x = 7a/5$ above the table.

It is therefore possible to eliminate the sliding phase of the motion of snooker or billiard balls if the ball is struck with a horizontal blow at a point whose height above the table is equal to 0.7 times the diameter of the ball. The cushions around the perimeter of the table are also set at this height so that a ball which rolls up to the cushion will rebound smoothly without skidding. Consequently it will only experience a small reduction in velocity due to the small loss of energy at impact.

The final level of mathematical analysis of ball games involves a study of the interaction between the separation effects of the flow (as shown in Fig. 6.3(a) and 6.3(b)), the size of the wake and consequent drag force experienced by the ball.

Fig. 7.13(a) shows the results of some wind tunnel tests conducted to measure the drag force experienced by a golf ball placed in an airstream of velocity v. The drag force increases according to a velocity squared law up to an airflow velocity of v_1. If the airflow velocity is increased above this value the drag force decreases until at a still higher velocity v_2 it begins to increase again. This strange behaviour suggests the existence of two different flow patterns, the distinction between them being the nature of the wake downstream of the ball. For low air speeds the air flows past the ball and the wake in an orderly fashion (this is called

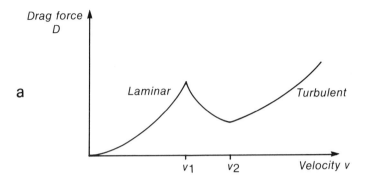

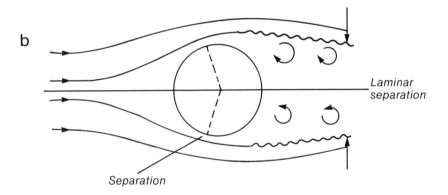

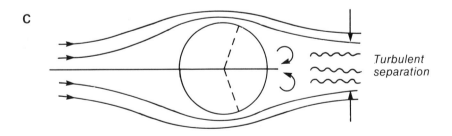

Fig. 7.13 – Diagrams to illustrate variation of drag force (D) with velocity (v), laminar and turbulent wakes.

laminar flow) but as the air speed increases it reaches a critical value at which sections of the flow become turbulent. The reduced drag in the case of the turbulent flow is explained by the fact that the turbulent flow helps to keep the air in contact with the surface of the ball for longer (see Fig. 7.13(b) and (c)), thus reducing the width of the wake and consequently the drag. It is thus apparent that the magnitude of the drag force experienced by the ball is dependent upon the position at which the separation of the flow from the surface of the ball occurs. It follows that if separation can be delayed the drag force experienced by the ball will be less. As already stated in Chapter 6 turbulence can be induced by roughening the surface; this is the reason for the dimpled surface of a golf ball. The dimples promote a turbulent air flow which in turn delays separation. Consequently the size of the wake is reduced (see Fig. 7.13(c)), and hence so too is the drag force. The result is that the range attained by the ball is dramatically increased; a swing which drives a dimpled ball some two hundred and fifty yards will only drive a smooth ball about fifty yards.

Fig. 7.13(a) can also be used to explain the sudden dip sometimes observed towards the end of a delivery by a fast bowler in a cricket match. Initially the ball is released at a high speed and experiences a drag force as a result of which it begins to slow down. If its speed falls below that required to maintain turbulence close to the ball, there will be a sudden increase in the magnitude of the drag force. This causes a sudden decrease in the velocity of the ball and hence a significant foreshortening of the ball's trajectory.

Apart from a study of the impacts between balls and the effects of spin and viscosity there are other interesting aspects of ball games which can be examined, for example

(i) forward passes in rugby football,
(ii) the effect of the wind on the motion of a ball.

7.5 FORWARD PASSES IN RUGBY FOOTBALL

The rules of the game of rugby football state that it is illegal to pass the ball forwards. 'A throw forward' is defined as 'the propulsion of the ball by hand or arm of a player in the direction of his opponent's dead ball line'. Although no mention is made of any reference point with respect to which the motion is to be measured, it is clear that the intention is to establish the illegality of any forward motion of the ball relative to some fixed reference point which in this case is the pitch. When a pass is made between two players, the player who passes the ball is generally moving forward so that the true velocity of the ball is given by the vector sum of the player's velocity and the relative velocity of the ball with respect to the player since

Relative velocity of ball with respect to player $= v_{ball} - v_{player}$.

Fig. 7.14 shows a typical pass of the ball from player P_1 to player P_2, both players being assumed to be running on parallel paths at the same speed v. The velocity triangle is shown in Fig. 7.14 where OA represents the velocity of player P_1 (relative to the ground). The relative velocity of the ball with respect to the player lies along AB where angle OAB $= \theta$. In order that the velocity of the ball relative to the ground does not have a forward component (as indicated for example by OC) then the vector representing this absolute velocity of the ball must be of magnitude OD or more.

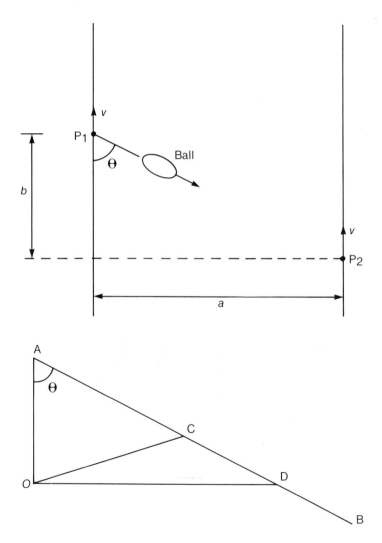

Fig. 7.14 – Rugby passes.

The minimum permitted magnitude of ball velocity relative to the player P_1 (represented by AD) is therefore given by

$$v \sec \theta = v \left(1 + \frac{a^2}{b^2} \right)^{\frac{1}{2}}.$$

Since typical dimensions for a rugby pass are $a = 5$ m, $b = 1$ m and $v = 5$ ms^{-1} it follows that a player must be capable of throwing a rugby ball relative to himself at a speed of approximately 25 ms^{-1}. Since this is approximately the speed at which a cricket ball leaves the hand of a fast bowler it follows that many of the passes allowed by referees infringe the regulations! The referee's decision is made even more difficult by the fact that he too is moving relative to both the players and the ball which further complicates the equations of relative motion. In the Scotland versus England rugby match in 1979, an English player made a forward pass which although undetected by the referee was blatantly obvious when seen on a television film of the game. The pass was made on one side of the 22 m line, the ball passed forwards across the line and was received by another player on the opposite side of the line. This occasion is mentioned not as criticism of the referee but to emphasize how difficult it is to judge a pass as being forward unless it happens to be made in the neighbourhood of a fixed reference mark, such as the 22 m line.

7.6 THE EFFECT OF THE WIND ON THE MOTION OF A BALL

In the absence of any air resistance or spin effects, once a ball has been kicked into the air or driven off a golf tee it continues along its parabolic trajectory until it lands. Generally a wind will be blowing so a more realistic picture of the motion of the ball will be obtained if allowance is made for this. Since the effects of a headwind (or tailwind) and a crosswind upon the motion of the ball are very different we shall consider each case separately.

Suppose the ball is driven off the ground with velocity U at an angle α to the horizontal, into a headwind of velocity W. From Fig. 7.15, the velocity of the ball relative to the wind is

$$v_{ball} - v_{wind}$$

$$= U \cos \alpha \, \mathbf{i} + U \sin \alpha \, \mathbf{j} - (-W\mathbf{i})$$

$$= (W + U \cos \alpha) \, \mathbf{i} + U \sin \alpha \, \mathbf{j}$$

The inclination of this velocity to the horizontal is given by θ where

$$\tan \theta = \frac{U \sin \alpha}{W + U \cos \alpha} \tag{7.9}$$

and its magnitude is

$$V = \sqrt{(U^2 + 2WU \cos \alpha + W^2)}. \tag{7.10}$$

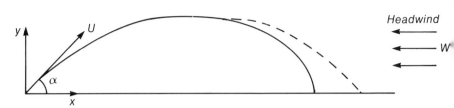

Fig. 7.15 – Diagram to illustrate notation used for determining the effect of a headwind on the ball's trajectory.

Equations (7.9) and (7.10) represent the motion of the ball relative to the air which throughout the time of flight T s has been moving in the negative x direction with speed W. A distance WT must therefore be subtracted from the range determined by equations (7.9) and (7.10) in order to give the range relative to the ground as

$$\frac{V^2 \sin 2\theta}{g} - WT.$$

For example, consider a soccer ball kicked at $45°$ to the ground with a velocity of 30 ms^{-1}. In the absence of wind, spin and air resistance effects the range of the kick is

$$\frac{30^2 \sin (2 \times 45°)}{9.81} = 91.74 \text{ m},$$

and the time of flight is given by

$$T = \frac{2V \sin \alpha}{g}$$

$$= \frac{2 \times 30 \times \sin 45°}{9.81} = 4.32 \text{ s}.$$

Suppose now that the kick was made into a headwind of 5 ms^{-1} then using equations (7.9) and (7.10)

$$V = \sqrt{(30^2 + 2 \times 30 \times 5 \times \cos 45° + 5^2)} = 33.72 \text{ ms}^{-1}$$

and

$$\theta = \text{arc tan} \left(\frac{30 \sin 45°}{5 + 30 \cos 45°} \right) = 38.98°,$$

The range when kicked into the headwind is therefore

$$\frac{33.72^2 \sin (2 \times 38.98°)}{9.81} - 6 \times 4.2 = 88.16 \text{ m},$$

assuming a time of flight of 4.2 s (i.e. slightly less than in still air). The effect of the headwind is thus to reduce the range of the kick, as you would expect. A following wind could be treated in exactly the same way.

Fig. 7.16 shows the soccer ball propelled from the origin with the same initial conditions as before but in the presence of a crosswind, at right-angles to the initial direction of the kick. Since the crosswind is at right angles to the xy plane it has little effect on the range of the kick but it does produce a deflection of the trajectory in the direction of the wind. To estimate the magnitude of this

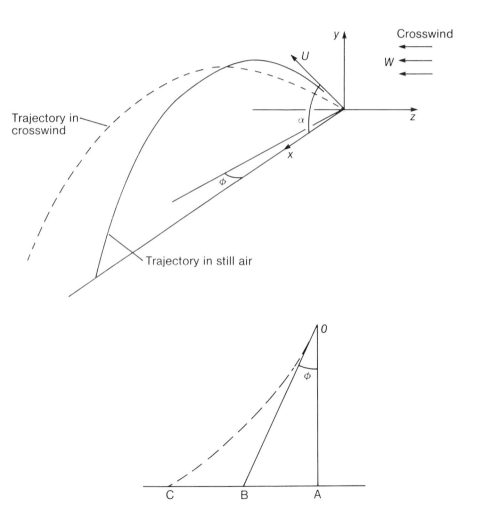

Fig. 7.16 – Diagrams to illustrate notation used for determining the effect of a crosswind on the ball's trajectory.

deflection, the motion of the ball relative to the wind is first determined and then allowance is made for the movement of the wind during the flight.

The velocity of the ball relative to the air is given by the vector difference

$$v_{ball} - v_{air}$$

$$= (U \cos \alpha \mathbf{i} + U \sin \alpha \mathbf{j}) - (-W\mathbf{k})$$

$$= U \cos \alpha \mathbf{i} + U \sin \alpha \mathbf{j} + W\mathbf{k} .$$

The angle ϕ between the plane of the trajectory in still air and the initial direction of the ball in the presence of the wind can be determined from the components of this vector as

$$\phi = \text{arc tan} \left(\frac{W}{U \cos \alpha} \right) .$$

Throughout the flight of the ball, the air is moving in the negative z direction with velocity W so that relative to the ground the motion of the ball is shown in Fig. 7.16. OA represents the direction in which the ball was propelled and OB represents the path of the ball relative to the air. During the flight of the ball the point B is carried across to C (the actual point where the ball lands) so that BC represents the deflection due to the wind.

Assuming OA represents the range R m in still air and the time of flight is T s then AC $= WT$ where W is the wind speed; the deflection due to the wind is thus given by

$$WT - R \tan \phi$$

$$= W \left(T - \frac{R}{U \cos \alpha} \right) .$$

For the data given earlier in this section the deflection of the kick due to the crosswind is thus

$$5 \left(5 - \frac{91.74}{30 \times \cos 45°} \right) = 3.38 \text{ m} ,$$

assuming a time of flight of 5 s (i.e. slightly longer than in still air).

It must be noted that the calculations presented in this section are purely illustrative. They are based on the assumptions of constant speed and direction of the wind whereas in fact the wind velocity near the ground is very variable. Nevertheless the results give an insight into the effects on the flight of a ball of headwinds and crosswinds.

You could estimate the effects of the same winds on a golf drive using the data that typical values of the velocity of projection and angle of projection of a tee shot are 70 ms^{-1} and 12° respectively.

7.7 CRICKET VERSUS BASEBALL – WHICH IS THE MORE DIFFICULT SPORT TO MASTER?

Although cricket and baseball each involve a bat–ball collision and are thus both governed by the same physical laws, there are many significant differences between the two games. Comparison of these similarities and differences may enable a decision to be reached as to which is the more difficult game to master. A similar analysis has been published by P. J. Brancazio in the *New Scientist* (22/29 December 1983).

Although the baseball pitcher throws the ball from a stationary position compared with the running delivery of a cricket bowler he is not constrained to deliver the ball with a straight- and over-arm action. This enables the pitcher to use more arm and shoulder muscles and thus give the ball a greater velocity and spin. Typical values for the release velocities and initial spin values are for baseball 37.5 ms^{-1} and 30 revolutions per second compared with the corresponding cricket values of 30 ms^{-1} and 10 revolutions per second. This implies that the Magnus force experienced by a baseball is greater than for a cricket ball. Consequently it is possible to swing a baseball further from its normal path than a cricket ball.

Earlier in this chapter it was explained that roughness of the surface of the ball promotes turbulence which in turn delays the separation of the air flow around the ball and so reduces the drag force on the ball. This is the reason why one often sees a bowler vigorously polish the ball on his clothes in order to make one side smoother than the other and so vary the magnitude of the drag force over the surface of the ball. The resulting force gradient can then be used to swing the ball in any chosen direction depending upon the orientation of the polished area. Although at one time such polishing was also permitted in baseball, it was exploited to such an extent by the pitcher that it was ultimately considered an unfair advantage and consequently the practice has been banned.

When a baseball is released by the pitcher, at 35 ms^{-1} say, it is some 18 m from the batter and so reaches him in about 0.5 s. A cricket ball is released approximately 20 m from the batsman and so, travelling at about 30 ms^{-1}, takes about 0.7 s to reach the batsman. The batsman thus has longer to decide upon his playing strategy. This advantage in favour of cricket is negated to some extent by the fact that a bowler is allowed to bounce the ball off the playing surface before it reaches the batsman whereas a pitcher is not. Since the cricket ball is spinning when it hits the ground then its direction will be changed by the impact and so make matters more difficult for the batsman, although he does have slightly longer to react since the impact also reduces the velocity of the ball.

One major difference in difficulty between the two sports arises at the impact between the bat and the ball. The cricket ball (of diameter 0.036 m) is hit by the cricket bat's plane face (of approximate width 0.11 m) whereas the baseball bat has a circular cross section of diameter 0.07 m with which to accurately hit the baseball so in this respect it could be said that a successful hit is easier in cricket. Furthermore a batsman can hit the ball in any direction he wishes whereas a batter must hit the ball forwards and within a sector of forty-five degrees either side of a line joining him to the pitcher. Since the batter attempts to do this by hitting a spherical ball with a cylindrical bat he has the more difficult task because there is a greater chance of a mishit.

Both the baseball bat and the cricket bat weigh a maximum of about 1.02 kg and are of comparable lengths (the maximum overall length of a cricket bat is 0.965 m and of a baseball bat 1.07 m). The mechanics of swinging the bat is thus similar for both games. In order to propel the ball with as great a velocity as possible we must decide whether to swing a light bat at high speed up to the moment of impact, or a heavier bat at a lower speed. A mathematical analysis of the collision between the bat and the ball reveals that more momentum is transferred to the ball by a bat which has a high speed (and thus a low weight) immediately prior to the impact. Light bats made of aluminium have been available to baseball players for a considerable time whereas the incidence of aluminium cricket bats is very low. The author is only aware of that used by the Australian cricketer Dennis Lillee in 1979. His experiment was short-lived as the cricket authorities banned its use because 'it damages the ball'. One wonders whether one day the cricket grounds of the world will echo to the metallic ring of the bat rather than to-day's sound of leather on willow!

In conclusion, there does not seem to be much to choose between the difficulties encountered in either game, each has its own advantages and disadvantages. The fact that no firm conclusion can be made from this discussion does not really matter, the important thing is that both games are enjoyed by thousands of people. It would make an interesting experiment to exchange a cricketer and a baseball player and see how each performed in the other's sport!

Appendix I: BASIC computer program for determining the moment of inertia of a runner's leg about a horizontal axis through the hip

During one stride the positions adopted by a runner's leg vary considerably. The leg positions of a sprinter and a middle distance runner during one stride are shown in Fig. 1.4. Throughout the stride, the rotation of the leg takes place about a horizontal axis drawn through the hip H and the only measurement which changes from one position to the next is the distance D from the hip to the centre of mass (G_2) of the lower leg and foot.

The BASIC program presented in this appendix computes the moment of inertia of the complete lower limb about a horizontal axis through the hip for each of the leg positions shown in Fig. 1.4. It is only necessary to input the mass of the athlete, the values of D, which can be obtained from Fig. 1.4 using the scale provided, and the radius and length of both the upper leg and the combined lower leg and foot.

As explained in Chapter 1 the complete limb is modelled as two circular cylinders as shown in Fig. 1.5. The cylinder representing the upper leg has a mass equal to $0.137 \times$ the total mass of the runner while the cylinder representing the lower leg and foot has a mass equal to $0.06 \times$ the total mass of the runner. The lengths of the two cylinders were obtained by measuring the distance from a subject's hip to the knee and from the knee to a point below the ankle bone (to make some allowance for the inclusion of the foot). Using himself as a subject the author obtained a length of 0.45 m for the upper 'cylinder' and 0.50 m for the lower 'cylinder'. (The values obtained will depend upon the physique of the subject.)

In order to determine the radius of each cylinder three circumferences were measured (at the top, the middle and bottom) of both the thigh and the lower leg and foot. The average circumference of each was determined and from these the radii of the upper (thigh) and lower cylinders (lower leg and foot) were obtained. Using himself as a subject the author obtained a radius of 0.07 m for the upper cylinder and 0.05 m for the lower cylinder. (Like the lengths, the values will depend on the physique of the subject.)

The program uses the result that for a cylinder of mass m, radius a and length h the moment of inertia I about an axis through the centre of mass and perpendicular to the length is given by

$$I = m\left(\frac{a^2}{4} + \frac{h^2}{12}\right).$$

Since the value of the moment of inertia must be obtained relative to the axis of rotation (the horizontal through the hip) the parallel axes theorem is used to obtain this from the moment of inertia about a parallel axis through the centre of mass of each cylinder.

The parallel axes theorem states that if I_H denotes the moment of inertia of the cylinder about the axis of rotation and I_G denotes the moment of inertia about a parallel axis through the centre of mass then

$$I_H = I_G + md^2,$$

where m is the mass of the cylinder and d is the perpendicular distance between the two axes.

Once you have weighed your subject (the subject used for obtaining Fig. 1.6 weighed 73 kg), measured the distance D from Fig. 1.4 and obtained your values for the radii and lengths of the cylinders, you can run the program. To input your data you simply respond to the various requests which are made in the program.

PROGRAM NAME: RUNNERLEG–MOI

```
100    PRINT "MOMENT OF INERTIA OF
       A"
200    PRINT "RUNNER'S LEG.ABOUT A"

300    PRINT "HORIZ. AXIS THRO'THE
       HIP."
400    PRINT "THE LEG IS TREATED AS
       TWO"
500    PRINT "CIRCULAR CYLINDERS,"
600    PRINT "1.UPPER LEG WITH C.OF
       M. G1"
700    PRINT "2.LOWER LEG AND FOOT
       WITH"
800    PRINT "  C.OF M. G2."
900    PRINT
1000   PRINT "TO ENTER YOUR DATA,R
       ESPOND"
1100   PRINT "TO THE VARIOUS REQUE
       STS."
1200   PRINT
1300   PRINT "HOW MANY DIFFERENT L
       EG"
1400   PRINT "POSNS. DO YOU WISH T
       O"
1500   PRINT "EXAMINE?"
```

```
1600   PRINT  "ENTER YOUR VALUE AND
       "
1700   PRINT  "PRESS RETURN."
1800   INPUT  N
1900   PRINT  "ANATOMICAL STUDIES S
       HOW"
2000   PRINT  "MASS OF UPPER LEG="
2100   PRINT  "          0.137*BOD
       Y WT."
2200   PRINT  "MASS OF LOWER LEG AN
       D"
2300   PRINT  "FOOT=0.06*BODY WT."
2400   PRINT  "WHAT IS BODY WT.(KG)
       OF"
2500   PRINT  "YOUR RUNNER?ENTER VA
       LUE"
2600   PRINT  "AND PRESS RETURN."
2700   INPUT  W
2800   PRINT  "WHAT ARE RADIUS(M) A
       ND"
2900   PRINT  "LENGTH(M) OF UPPER L
       EG"
3000   PRINT  "CYLINDER?ENTER VALUE
       S IN"
3100   PRINT  "THE ABOVE ORDER SEPA
       RATED"
3200   PRINT  "BY A COMMA,PRESS RET
       URN."
3300   INPUT  R1,L1
3400   PRINT  "WHAT ARE RADIUS(M) A
       ND"
3500   PRINT  "LENGTH(M) OF LOWER L
       EG"
3600   PRINT  "AND FOOT CYLINDER?EN
       TER"
3700   PRINT  "VALUES IN THE ABOVE
       ORDER"
3800   PRINT  "SEP. BY COMMA,PRESS
       RETURN"
3900   INPUT  R2,L2
4000   PRINT  "WHEN CURSOR FLASHES
       ENTER"
4100   PRINT  "YOUR FIRST VALUE OF
       D (SEE"
4200   PRINT  "TEXT) AND PRESS RETU
       RN."
4300   PRINT  "WHEN CURSOR REAPPEAR
       S ENTER"
```

```
4400   PRINT "NEXT D VALUE UNTIL A
       LL USED."
4500   GOSUB 8300
4700   PRINT "MASS OF RUNNER(KG)="
       ;W
4800   PRINT
4900   PRINT "UPPER LEG- MASS(KG)=
       ";W1
5000   PRINT "          RADIUS(M) =
       ";R1
5100   PRINT "          LENGTH(M) =
       ";L1
5120   PRINT "LOWER LEG AND FOOT-"

5130   PRINT "          MASS(KG)="
       ;W2
5140   PRINT "          RADIUS(M) =
       ";R2
5160   PRINT "          LENGTH(M) =
       ";L2
5200   PRINT
5500   PRINT
5600   PRINT "D(M)      LEG POS      M
       I(KGM^2)"
5900   FOR J = 1 TO N STEP 1
6000   REM   ENTER VALUE OF D CORRE
       S TO LEG
6100   REM   POSN J AND PRESS RETUR
       N.
6200   PRINT
6300   INPUT D
6400   REM   THE PROG NOW CALCULATE
       S THE
6500   REM   M. OF I.OF THE COMPLET
       E LEG
6600   REM   ABOUT HORIZ AXIS THRO
       HIPS.
6700   MI = I1 + C2 + W2 * (D ^ 2)
6900   PRINT D; TAB( 10);J; TAB( 1
       8);MI
7200   NEXT J
7300   GOTO 9999
7400   REM   SUBROUTINE CYLMOFI
7500   REM   THIS COMPUTES C1 THE M
       .OF I.
7600   REM   OF UPPER CYL ABOUT AXI
       S THRO
```

```
7700   REM   G1(C.OF M)PERP TO LENG
       TH AND
7800   REM   C2,CORRES M.OF I.FOR L
       OWER
7900   REM   LEG AND FOOT.PARALLEL
       AXES THM.
8000   REM   IS THEN USED TO CALC M
       .OF I.OF
8100   REM   UPPER LEG CYLINDER ABO
       UT
8200   REM   PARALLEL AXIS THRO HIP
       S.
8300   W1 = 0.137 * W
8400   C1 = W1 * ((R1 ^ 2) / 4.0 +
       (L1 ^ 2) / 12.0)
8500   W2 = 0.06 * W
8600   C2 = W2 * ((R2 ^ 2) / 4.0 +
       (L1 ^ 2) / 12.0)
8700   I1 = C1 + W1 * (L1 / 2.0) ^
       2
8800   RETURN
9999   END
```

Appendix I

Results based on leg shown in Fig. 1.4

```
MASS OF RUNNER(KG)=73

UPPER LEG- MASS(KG)=10.001
          RADIUS(M) =.07
          LENGTH(M) =.45
LOWER LEG AND FOOT-
          MASS(KG)=4.38
          RADIUS(M) =.05
          LENGTH(M) =.5


D(M)      LEG POS      MI(KGM^2)

.34          1          1.27029673

.62          2          2.44764073

.65          3          2.61451873

.64          4          2.55801673

.6           5          2.34076873

.51          6          1.90320673

.39          7          1.43016673

.47          8          1.73151073
```

Appendix II: BASIC computer program for determining the length of the throw or long jump for the shot put, hammer throw and long jump events

The range R of a projectile throw has been established elsewhere as

$$R = \frac{V^2 \cos A}{g} \left[\sin A + \sqrt{\left(\sin^2 A + \frac{2gH}{V^2} \right)} \right],$$

where V denotes the release velocity of the object, A the release angle, H the difference between the vertical displacements of the object at release and at landing and g is the acceleration due to gravity. This appendix contains a BASIC program which can be used to investigate the effect on R of varying any one of the release parameters H, V or A.

You should only vary one parameter at a time; if you vary more than one at a time you will be unable to decide how much of the consequent variation in the range can be attributed to each parameter. Your experiments with the program will reveal that variation in the release velocity has the most dramatic effect on the range. This could have been deduced from the expression for the range R since in this the release velocity V is squared and hence the effect of any change in V is magnified.

The shot put, hammer throw and long jump can each be analysed using this projectile model. In order that any conclusions from your analyses will be realistic the following table gives the range of values of the various parameters as recorded by elite athletes. The current world records are included for comparison purposes.

	Range of values of release height (m)	Range of values of release angle (deg)	Range of values of release velocity (ms^{-1})	World Record (m)
Shot put	1.8–2.5	40–45	10–14	22.15
Hammer	1.4–2.2	40–45	20–26	83.98
Long jump	0.4–0.6†	18–22	8–10	8.90

†These values refer to the change in vertical displacement of the athlete's centre of mass between take-off and landing. Also, in the case of the long jump, remember that the value obtained for R only refers to the projectile phase of the jump and is not equal to the length of the jump.

It is because greatest changes in the range R are caused by changes in the release velocity V that athletics coaches concentrate on improving an athlete's release velocity when coaching any of the throwing events.

PROGRAM NAME: LJTHROWS

```
10   PRINT "SPORTS TRAJECTORIES"
20   PRINT "THIS PACKAGE CONTAINS
     3 PROGS"
30   PRINT "FOR CALCULATING THE RA
     NGE OF"
40   PRINT "THE SHOTPUT,HAMMERTHRO
     W AND"
50   PRINT "THE LONGJUMP."
60   PRINT
70   PRINT "SELECT YOUR EVENT FROM
     MENU:"
80   PRINT "      1.SHOT"
90   PRINT "      2.HAMMER"
100  PRINT "      3.LONGJUMP"
110  PRINT "      4.EXIT(LEAVE PROG
     RAM)"
120  PRINT "ENTER VALUE CORRES. T
     O YOUR"
130  PRINT "CHOICE,PRESS RETURN"
140  INPUT N
150  IF N = 1 GOTO 210
160  IF N = 2 GOTO 530
170  IF N = 3 GOTO 850
180  IF N = 4 GOTO 9999
190  IF N > 4 GOTO 70
210  PRINT
220  PRINT "CALCULATION OF RANGE
     R(M) OF"
230  PRINT "SHOTPUT RELEASED WITH
     VEL."
240  PRINT "V(MS-1) AT AN ANGLE A
     (DEG)"
250  PRINT "TO HORIZ FROM A HEIGH
     T OF"
260  PRINT "H(M) ABOVE GROUNDLEVE
     L."
270  PRINT
290  PRINT "SELECT VALUES OF H,A,
     V FROM"
300  PRINT "TABLE GIVEN IN APPEND
     IX.ENTER"
310  PRINT "VALUES IN ABOVE ORDER
     SEPARATED"
320  PRINT "BY COMMAS AND PRESS R
     ETURN."
```

```
330    INPUT  H,A,V
340    GOSUB  1470
360    PRINT  "REL.VEL.  V=";V;"(MS-1
       )"
370    PRINT  "REL.ANGLE  A=";A;"(DEG
       )"
380    PRINT  "REL.HT.  H=";H;"(M)"
390    PRINT
400    PRINT  "RANGE  OF  SHOTPUT=";R;
       "(M)"
410    PRINT
420    PRINT  "FOR  COMPARISON  PURPOS
       ES,"
430    PRINT  "   WORLD  RECORD=22.15M
       ."
450    PRINT
460    PRINT  "DO  YOU  WANT  ANOTHER  T
       HROW?"
470    PRINT  "ANSWER  YES/NO,AND  PRE
       SS"
480    PRINT  "RETURN."
490    INPUT  K$
500    IF  K$  =  "YES"  GOTO  290
510    IF  K$  =  "NO"  GOTO  70
530    PRINT
540    PRINT  "CALCULATION  OF  THE  RA
       NGE  R"
550    PRINT  "(M)  OF  A  HAMMERTHROW,
       "
560    PRINT  "RELEASED  AT  V(MS-1)  A
       T  A(DEG)"
570    PRINT  "TO  HORIZ  FROM  HT.  H(M
       )  ABOVE"
580    PRINT  "GROUNDLEVEL."
590    PRINT
610    PRINT  "SELECT  VALUES  OF  H,A,
       V  FROM"
620    PRINT  "TABLE  IN  APPENDIX.ENT
       ER  THEM"
630    PRINT  "IN  ABOVE  ORDER  SEPARA
       TED  BY"
640    PRINT  "COMMAS  AND  PRESS  RETU
       RN."
650    INPUT  H,A,V
660    GOSUB  1470
680    PRINT
690    PRINT  "REL.VEL.V=";V;"(MS-1)
       "
```

```
700    PRINT "REL.ANGLE A=";A;"(DEG
       )"
710    PRINT "REL.HT. H=";H;"(M)"
720    PRINT
730    PRINT "RANGE OF HAMMERTHROW=
       ";R;"(M)"
740    PRINT
750    PRINT "FOR COMPARISON PURPOS
       ES."
760    PRINT "  WORLD RECORD=83.98M
       "
780    PRINT
790    PRINT "DO YOU WANT ANOTHER T
       HROW?"
810    INPUT L$
820    IF L$ = "YES" GOTO 610
830    IF L$ = "NO" GOTO 70
850    PRINT
860    PRINT "CALCN.OF RANGE OF AIR
       BORN"
870    PRINT "PHASE OF LONGJUMP,WIT
       H"
880    PRINT "TAKEOFF VEL.V,TAKEOFF
        ANGLE A"
890    PRINT "AND WHERE H DENOTES T
       HE CHANGE"
900    PRINT "IN VERT.DISP.OF C.OF
       M.BETWEEN"
910    PRINT "TAKEOFF AND LANDING."

920    PRINT "TO OBTAIN LENGTH OF J
       UMP YOU"
930    PRINT "MUST ADD ON THE DISTA
       NCES T AND L WHERE"
940    PRINT "T=HORIZ DIST C OF M I
       S AHEAD"
950    PRINT "  OF T-OFF BOARD AT T
       -OFF,"
960    PRINT "L=HORIZ DIST C OF M I
       S BEHIND"
970    PRINT "  HEELS ON LANDING."
980    PRINT
990    PRINT
1010   PRINT "SELECT VALUES OF H,A
       ,V FROM"
1020   PRINT "TABLE IN APPENDIX.EN
       TER"
```

```
1030   PRINT "THEM IN THAT ORDER S
       EPARATED"
1040   PRINT "BY COMMAS AND PRESS
       RETURN. "
1050   INPUT H,A,V
1070   PRINT
1080   PRINT "BEFORE LENGTH OF JUM
       P CAN BE"
1090   PRINT "FOUND,YOU NEED VALUE
       S OF T &L"
1100   PRINT "TYPICAL RANGES ARE: "

1110   PRINT "     T: 0.0-0.4M"
1120   PRINT "     L:0.75-1.00M"
1130   PRINT
1150   PRINT "SELECT VALUES OF T A
       ND L, "
1160   PRINT "ENTER THEM IN THAT O
       RDER"
1170   PRINT "SEPARATED BY COMMAS
       AND"
1180   PRINT "PRESS RETURN. "
1190   INPUT T,L
1200   GOSUB 1470
1210   REM   ONCE RANGE R HAS BEEN
       FOUND WE
1220   REM   ADD ON THE VALUES OF T
       & L TO
1230   REM   GIVE LENGTH OF LONGJUM
       P AS
1240   REM          LJ=T+R+L
1250 LJ = T + R + L
1270   PRINT
1280   PRINT "TAKEOFF VEL.V=";V;"(
       MS-1)"
1290   PRINT "T-OFF ANGLE A=";A;"(
       DEG)"
1300   PRINT "VERT DISP OF C OF M"

1310   PRINT "BETWEEN T/O&LANDING=
       ";H;"(M)"
1320   PRINT "VALUE OF T=";T;"(M)"

1330   PRINT "VALUE OF L=";L;"(M)"

1340   PRINT
1350   PRINT "LENGTH OF LONGJUMP="
       ;LJ;"(M)"
```

```
1360  PRINT
1370  PRINT "FOR COMPARISON PURPO
      SES,"
1380  PRINT "  WORLD RECORD=8.90M
      "
1390  PRINT
1410  PRINT "DO YOU WANT ANOTHER
      JUMP?"
1420  PRINT "ANSWER YES/NO,PRESS
      RETURN"
1430  INPUT M$
1440  IF M$ = "YES" GOTO 1010
1450  IF M$ = "NO" GOTO 70
1460  REM  SUBROUTINE RANGE R
1470  B = A * 3.14159 / 180.0
1480  G = 9.81
1490  D = ( SIN (B)) ^ 2 + (2.0 *
      G * H) / (V ^ 2)
1500  C =  SIN (B) +  SQR (D)
1510  R = (V ^ 2) * ( COS (B)) * C
      / G
1520  RETURN
9999  END
```

Results

```
CALCULATION OF RANGE R(M) OF
SHOTPUT RELEASED WITH VEL.
V(MS-1) AT AN ANGLE A(DEG)
TO HORIZ FROM A HEIGHT OF
H(M) ABOVE GROUNDLEVEL.


REL.VEL.  V=12.9(MS-1)
REL.ANGLE A=42(DEG)
REL.HT.  H=2(M)

RANGE OF SHOTPUT=18.8575341(M)

FOR COMPARISON PURPOSES,
  WORLD RECORD=22.15M.

REL.VEL.  V=13(MS-1)
REL.ANGLE A=42(DEG)
REL.HT.  H=2(M)

RANGE OF SHOTPUT=19.1230155(M)

FOR COMPARISON PURPOSES,
  WORLD RECORD=22.15M.


REL.VEL.  V=13.1(MS-1)
REL.ANGLE A=42(DEG)
REL.HT.  H=2(M)

RANGE OF SHOTPUT=19.3904737(M)

FOR COMPARISON PURPOSES,
  WORLD RECORD=22.15M.
```

```
CALCULATION OF THE RANGE R
(M) OF A HAMMERTHROW,
RELEASED AT V(MS-1) AT A(DEG)
TO HORIZ FROM HT. H(M) ABOVE
GROUNDLEVEL.


REL.VEL.V=24(MS-1)
REL.ANGLE A=42(DEG)
REL.HT. H=2(M)

RANGE OF HAMMERTHROW=60.536549(M)

FOR COMPARISON PURPOSES,
    WORLD RECORD=83.98M


REL.VEL.V=24(MS-1)
REL.ANGLE A=43(DEG)
REL.HT. H=2(M)

RANGE OF HAMMERTHROW=60.644043(M)

FOR COMPARISON PURPOSES,
    WORLD RECORD=83.98M


REL.VEL.V=24(MS-1)
REL.ANGLE A=44(DEG)
REL.HT. H=2(M)

RANGE OF HAMMERTHROW=60.6825376(M)

FOR COMPARISON PURPOSES,
    WORLD RECORD=83.98M
```

```
CALCN.OF RANGE OF AIRBORN
PHASE OF LONGJUMP,WITH
TAKEOFF VEL.V,TAKEOFF ANGLE A
AND WHERE H DENOTES THE CHANGE
IN VERT.DISP.OF C.OF M.BETWEEN
TAKEOFF AND LANDING.
TO OBTAIN LENGTH OF JUMP YOU
MUST ADD ON THE DISTANCES T AND L WHERE
T=HORIZ DIST C OF M IS AHEAD
   OF T-OFF BOARD AT T-OFF,
L=HORIZ DIST C OF M IS BEHIND
   HEELS ON LANDING.


BEFORE LENGTH OF JUMP CAN BE
FOUND,YOU NEED VALUES OF T &L
TYPICAL RANGES ARE:
   T: 0.0-0.4M
   L:0.75-1.00M


TAKEOFF VEL.V=8.5(MS-1)
T-OFF ANGLE A=20(DEG)
VERT DISP OF C OF M
BETWEEN T/O&LANDING=.5(M)
VALUE OF T=.3(M)
VALUE OF L=.75(M)

LENGTH OF LONGJUMP=6.89645205(M)

FOR COMPARISON PURPOSES,
   WORLD RECORD=8.90M



TAKEOFF VEL.V=9(MS-1)
T-OFF ANGLE A=20(DEG)
VERT DISP OF C OF M
BETWEEN T/O&LANDING=.5(M)
VALUE OF T=.3(M)
VALUE OF L=.75(M)

LENGTH OF LONGJUMP=7.48962701(M)

FOR COMPARISON PURPOSES,
   WORLD RECORD=8.90M
```

Appendix III: BASIC computer program for determining the optimum angle of projection of the shot, hammer or long jumper and subsequent calculation of the resulting range

The angle of release A corresponding to maximum range R for a projectile released from a height h m above ground level with a velocity V ms^{-1} is given by

$$\cos 2A = \frac{gh}{V^2 + gh} \quad,$$

where g denotes the acceleration due to gravity.

The value of the maximum range can then be calculated from

$$R = \frac{V^2 \cos A}{g} \left[\sin A + \sqrt{\left(\sin^2 A + \frac{2gh}{V^2} \right)} \right] .$$

Since A depends on h and V it is of interest to investigate how both it and the maximum range R vary when either h is varied (for a fixed V) or V is varied (for a fixed h). Do not attempt to vary h and V simultaneously since you will be unable to identify how much of the variation in R is due to h and how much is due to V! In order that your results will be realistic the range of values for release height and release velocity for the shot put, hammer throw and long jump are given below.

	Range of values of release height (m)	Range of values of release velocity (V ms^{-1})
Shot put	1.8–2.5	10–14
Hammer	1.4–2.2	20–26
Long jump	0.4–0.6†	8–10

†These values refer to the change in vertical displacement of the athlete's centre of mass between take-off and landing. Also, in the case of the long jump remember that the value obtained for R only refers to the projectile phase of the jump and is not equal to the length of the jump.

With the following coding you can investigate the effect on the optimum release angle and the resulting range of either

(1) fixing the release height and varying the release velocity or
(2) fixing the release velocity and varying the release height.

A sample output of the program is included. Inspection shows that the range is affected to a much greater extent by variations in the release velocity. This result could have been predicted from the expression for the range since it involves the square of the release velocity and consequently any changes in V have their effects squared.

PROGRAM NAME: OPTIRELANGLE

```
10   PRINT "OPTIMUM RELEASE ANGLE
     FOR THE"
20   PRINT "THROWS AND LONG JUMP"
40   PRINT
50   PRINT "AN INVESTIGATION INTO
     THE"
60   PRINT "EFFECT OF VARYING RELE
     ASE"
70   PRINT "HEIGHT OR RELEASE VELO
     CITY"
80   PRINT "ON THE OPTIMUM ANGLE O
     F"
90   PRINT "RELEASE/TAKEOFF NEEDED
     TO"
100  PRINT "MAXIMISE THE RANGE IN
     THE"
110  PRINT "SHOT,HAMMER OR LONGJU
     MP."
120  PRINT
130  PRINT "THIS PROG. COMPUTES T
     HE"
140  PRINT "REL.ANGLE A(DEG) NEED
     ED TO"
150  PRINT "MAXIMISE THE RANGE FO
     R"
160  PRINT "GIVEN VALUES OF REL.H
     T.H(M)"
170  PRINT "AND RELEASE VEL. V(MS
     -1)."
190  PRINT "WHEN YOU ARE READY TO
     CONTINUE"
200  PRINT "ENTER Y AND PRESS RET
     URN."
210  INPUT M$
220  IF M$ = "Y" GOTO 260
230  PRINT
260  PRINT "YOU CAN ELECT EITHER
     TO:"
```

```
270    PRINT "1.FIX H AND VARY V."
280    PRINT "   THE OUTPUT WILL SHO
       W THE"
290    PRINT "   VALUE OF H AND PRES
       ENT THE"
300    PRINT "   VALUES OF V,A,RANGE
       IN A TABLE."
310    PRINT "OR"
320    PRINT "2.FIX V AND VARY H."
330    PRINT "   THE OUTPUT WILL SHO
       W THE "
340    PRINT "   VALUE OF V AND PRES
       ENT"
350    PRINT "   H,A,RANGE IN A TABL
       E."
360    PRINT
380    PRINT "SELECT YOUR OPTION 1
       OR 2:"
390    PRINT "ENTER 1 OR 2,PRESS RE
       TURN."
400    INPUT M
410    IF M = 1 GOTO 460
420    IF M = 2 GOTO 780
430    IF M > 2 GOTO 380
440    PRINT
450    PRINT
460    PRINT "WHAT IS YOUR (FIXED)
       VALUE"
470    PRINT "OF REL.HT. H(M)?"
480    PRINT "ENTER VALUE,PRESS RET
       URN."
490    INPUT H
500    PRINT "HOW MANY VALUES OF RE
       L.VEL."
510    PRINT "DO YOU WANT TO TRY?"
520    PRINT "ENTER VALUE,PRESS RET
       URN."
530    INPUT K
550    PRINT
560    PRINT
570    PRINT "REL.HEIGHT H(M)=";H
580    PRINT "V=RELEASE VELOCITY (M
       S-1)"
590    PRINT "A=REL./TAKEOFF ANGLE(
       DEG)"
600    PRINT "R=MAX. RANGE"
610    PRINT "V(MS-1)         A(DEG)
                 R(M)"
```

```
630   FOR I = 1 TO K STEP 1
640   PRINT "ENTER VALUE OF REL.VE
      L. IN"
650   PRINT "MS-1,PRESS RETURN."
660   INPUT V
670   GOSUB 1160
690   PRINT V; TAB( 10);A; TAB( 25
      );R
710   NEXT I
720   PRINT "DO YOU WISH TO TRY TH
      E OTHER"
730   PRINT "EXPT ? ANSWER YES/NO
      AND"
740   PRINT "PRESS RETURN."
750   INPUT K$
760   IF K$ = "YES" GOTO 780
770   IF K$ = "NO" GOTO 9999
780   PRINT "WHAT IS YOUR (FIXED)
      VALUE"
790   PRINT "OF REL.VELOCITY (MS-1
      )?"
800   PRINT "ENTER VALUE,PRESS RET
      URN."
810   INPUT V
820   PRINT "HOW MANY VALUES OF RE
      LEASE"
830   PRINT "HT.(M) DO YOU WANT TO
      TRY?"
840   PRINT "ENTER VALUE,PRESS RET
      URN."
850   INPUT N
870   PRINT
880   PRINT
890   PRINT "RELEASE VEL V(MS-1)="
      ;V
900   PRINT "H=RELEASE HEIGHT(M)"
910   PRINT "A=OPT.REL./TAKEOFF AN
      GLE(DEG)"
920   PRINT "H(M)          A(DEG)
                R(M)"
940   FOR J = 1 TO N STEP 1
950   PRINT "ENTER VALUE OF REL.HT
      .(M)"
960   PRINT "AND PRESS RETURN."
970   INPUT H
980   GOSUB 1160
1000  PRINT H; TAB( 10);A; TAB( 2
      5);R
```

```
1020   NEXT J
1030   PRINT "DO YOU WISH TO TRY T
       HE"
1040   PRINT "OTHER EXPT.? ANSWER
       YES/NO"
1050   PRINT "AND PRESS RETURN."
1060   PRINT
1070   INPUT L$
1080   IF L$ = "YES" GOTO 460
1090   IF L$ = "NO" GOTO 9999
1100   REM   THIS SUBROUTINE COMPUT
       ES THE
1110   REM   OPTIMUM REL.ANG.(A DEG
       ) AND
1120   REM   THE RESULTING RANGE (R
       M) FOR
1130   REM   GIVEN VALUES OF RELEAS
       E HT.(H M)
1140   REM   AND RELEASE VELOCITY (
       V MS-1).
1150   REM   SUBROUTINE OPTARMX
1160   G = 9.81
1170   F = V ^ 2 + (G * H)
1180   C = (G * H) / F
1190   S = (1.0 - (C ^ 2)) ^ 0.5
1200   B = 0.5 *  ATN (S / C)
1210   A = B * 180.0 / 3.14159
1220   P = ( SIN (B)) ^ 2 + ((2 * G
        * H) / (V ^ 2))
1230   Q =  SIN (B) + P ^ 0.5
1240   R = (V ^ 2) * ( COS (B)) * Q
        / G
1250   RETURN
9999   END
```

Results

```
AN INVESTIGATION INTO THE
EFFECT OF VARYING RELEASE
HEIGHT OR RELEASE VELOCITY
ON THE OPTIMUM ANGLE OF
RELEASE/TAKEOFF NEEDED TO
MAXIMISE THE RANGE IN THE
SHOT,HAMMER OR LONGJUMP.

THIS PROG. COMPUTES THE
REL.ANGLE A(DEG) NEEDED TO
MAXIMISE THE RANGE FOR
GIVEN VALUES OF REL.HT.H(M)
AND RELEASE VEL. V(MS-1).


YOU CAN ELECT EITHER TO:
1.FIX H AND VARY V.
   THE OUTPUT WILL SHOW THE
   VALUE OF H AND PRESENT THE
   VALUES OF V,A,RANGE IN A TABLE.
OR
2.FIX V AND VARY H.
   THE OUTPUT WILL SHOW THE
   VALUE OF V AND PRESENT
   H,A,RANGE IN A TABLE.


REL.HEIGHT H(M)=2
V=RELEASE VELOCITY (MS-1)
A=REL./TAKEOFF ANGLE(DEG)
R=MAX. RANGE
```

V(MS-1)	A(DEG)	R(M)
10		
10	40.2798971	12.0285423
11		
11	40.9898553	14.194142
12		
12	41.5565234	16.5585529
13		
13	42.0147203	19.1230175
14		
14	42.3896558	21.8884301

```
RELEASE  VEL  V(MS-1)=13
H=RELEASE  HEIGHT(M)
A=OPT.REL./TAKEOFF  ANGLE(DEG)
H(M)         A(DEG)                  R(M)
  1.8
1.8       42.2858632      18.941987
  2.0
2         42.0147203      19.1230175
  2.2
2.2       41.7488998      19.3023503
  2.4
2.4       41.488224       19.4800322
  2.5
2.5       41.3597621      19.5682681
```

Appendix IV: BASIC computer program for determining the success or failure of a basketball free throw

As with many other sports examples, a free throw in basketball can be analysed by using a standard projectile treatment.

It is explained in the text that not only must the player ensure that the trajectory of the ball passes through the hoop (for simplicity centre to centre passage is assumed) but also that when the ball arrives at the hoop its angle of approach is suitable for entry.

For a given release velocity V ms^{-1} the angle of release A for centre to centre passage is given by

$$\tan A = \frac{V^2}{gx_1} \left[1 \pm \sqrt{\left(1 - \frac{2g}{V^2}\left(y_1 + \frac{gx_1^2}{2V^2}\right)\right)} \right],$$

where (x_1, y_1) are the coordinates of the hoop referred to an origin of coordinates at the centre of the basketball at the moment of release. (The analysis is developed in terms of a fixed value of V since skilled basketball players consider that V is more easily replicated than α).

The BASIC program presented in this appendix computes the two values of A from the above equation after you have input values for V and H, the height above ground level of the basketball centre at the moment of release.

The two values of A are then used to determine the corresponding angle of entry B to the hoop from

$$B = -\arctan\left(\frac{dy}{dx}\right)_{(x_1, y_1)},$$

where the equation of the trajectory of the basketball is

$$y = x \tan A - \frac{gx^2}{2V^2} \sec^2 A.$$

It was established in the text that passage of the ball through the hoop is not possible unless

$$B > 33.14°.$$

Finally the program tests your two values of B against this critical value and prints out a suitable message, dependent upon your basketball skill! Since a player may be awarded more than one free throw, the program contains an option for you to have additional throws.

To input your data (the values of V and H) you simply respond to the various requests which are made in the program. You can either experiment with arbitrary values of V and H (which may not give a suitable trajectory) or alternatively select values from amongst the following reasonable ranges.

$V(\text{ms}^{-1})$: 6 – 9 ms^{-1}

$H(\text{m})$: 2.0–2.5 m

The relevant dimensions of a basketball court are shown in Fig. A.1 and A.2.

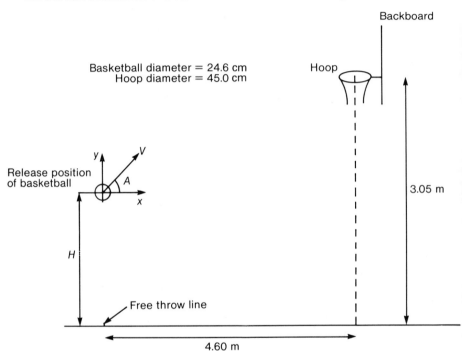

Fig. A1 – Dimensions involved in a free throw.

$d = 45 \sin B$

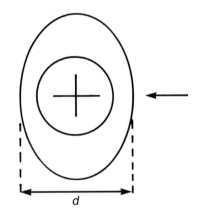

Fig. A2 – Entry to the hoop.

PROGRAM NAME: B/BALLFREETHROW

```
10    PRINT "BASKETBALL FREE THROWS
      "
20    PRINT
40    PRINT "THIS PROGRAM TESTS WHE
      THER"
50    PRINT "A BASKETBALL FREE THRO
      W WILL"
60    PRINT "BE SUCCESSFUL."
70    PRINT "YOU NEED ONLY INPUT A
      VALUE"
80    PRINT "OF RELEASE VELOCITY V(
      MS-1)"
90    PRINT "AND REL.HEIGHT H(M)."
100   PRINT
110   PRINT "THE PROGRAM COMPUTES
      THE TWO"
120   PRINT "RESULTING RELEASE ANG
      LES A1"
130   PRINT "AND A2 (DEG) FOR WHIC
      H THE"
140   PRINT "CENTRE OF THE BALL WI
      LL PASS"
150   PRINT "THROUGH THE CENTRE OF
      THE HOOP"
160   PRINT
170   PRINT
180   PRINT "THESE TWO RELEASE ANG
      LES ARE"
190   PRINT "THEN USED TO CALC. B1
      AND B2"
200   PRINT "(DEG),THE CONSEQUENT
      ANGLES OF"
210   PRINT "ATTEMPTED ENTRY TO TH
      E HOOP."
220   PRINT
240   PRINT
250   PRINT "WHEN YOU ARE READY TO
      CONTINUE"
260   PRINT "ENTER Y AND PRESS RET
      URN."
270   INPUT M$
280   IF M$ = "Y" GOTO 310
290   PRINT
310   PRINT
```

```
320    PRINT "THE GEOMETRY OF BALL
       ENTRY TO"
330    PRINT "HOOP SHOWS THAT ENTRY
       IS"
340    PRINT "IMPOSSIBLE UNLESS"
350    PRINT "  ANGLE OF ENTRY>33.1
       4 DEG."
360    PRINT
370    PRINT "WHATEVER THE OUTCOME
       OF YOUR"
380    PRINT "FREE THROW,A SUITABLE
       MESSAGE"
390    PRINT "IS PRINTED!"
410    PRINT
420    PRINT "WHAT IS REL.VEL.(MS-1
       ) OF"
430    PRINT "BASKETBALL?"
440    PRINT "SENSIBLE RANGE: 6-9 M
       S-1."
450    PRINT "ENTER VALUE,PRESS RET
       URN."
460    INPUT V
470    PRINT "WHAT IS REL.HT.(M) OF
       "
480    PRINT "BASKETBALL?"
490    PRINT "SENSIBLE RANGE:2.0-2.
       75 M."
500    PRINT "ENTER VALUE,PRESS RET
       URN."
510    INPUT H
520    X = 4.60
530    Y = 3.05 - H
540    G = 9.81
550    S = Y + G * (X ^ 2) / (2.0 *
       (V ^ 2))
560    T = 1.0 - 2.0 * G * S / (V ^
       2)
570    IF T < 0.0 THEN 1070
573    REM  THIS TESTS FOR SQUARE R
       OOT OF
576    REM  NEG. NO. IN TAN(A) EXPR
       ESSION.
580    D1 = 1.0 +  SQR (T)
590    D2 = 1.0 -  SQR (T)
600    E1 = (V ^ 2) * D1 / (G * X)
610    E2 = (V ^ 2) * D2 / (G * X)
620    A1 = ( ATN (E1)) * 180.0 / 3.
       14159
```

```
630 A2 = ( ATN (E2)) * 180.0 / 3.
    14159
640 F1 =   TAN (A1) - (G * X) / ((
    V *  COS (A1)) ^ 2)
650 F2 =   TAN (A2) - (G * X) / ((
    V *  COS (A2)) ^ 2)
660 B1 =  - ( ATN (F1)) * 180.0 /
    3.14159
670 B2 =  - ( ATN (F2)) * 180.0 /
    3.14159
680 PRINT
700 PRINT
710 PRINT
720 PRINT "FOR REL.VEL.V(MS-1)="
    ;V
730 PRINT "AND REL.HT. H(M)=";H
740 PRINT
750 PRINT "THE TWO POSS.REL.ANG.
    ARE"
760 PRINT
770 PRINT "A1(DEG)=";A1;"A2(DEG)
    =";A2
780 PRINT
790 PRINT "THE TWO ASSOC.ANGLES
    OF"
800 PRINT "ENTRY ARE"
810 PRINT
820 PRINT "B1(DEG)=";B1;"B2(DEG)
    =";B2
840 PRINT
850 IF B1 < 33.14 THEN 870
860 IF B1 >  = 33.14 THEN 960
870 IF B2 < 33.14 THEN 900
880 IF B2 >  = 33.14 THEN 960
900 PRINT
910 PRINT "BAD LUCK-YOU MISSED-N
    O POINTS!"
920 PRINT
940 GOTO 1000
960 PRINT
970 PRINT "GREAT SHOT-YOU SCORED
    !"
980 PRINT
1000 PRINT "DO YOU WANT ANOTHER
    THROW?"
1010 PRINT "ANSWER YES/NO,PRESS
    RETURN."
1020 INPUT K$
```

```
1030   IF K$ = "YES" GOTO 420
1040   IF K$ = "NO" GOTO 9999
1070   PRINT
1080   PRINT "TRY DIFFERENT VALUES
       OF V"
1090   PRINT "AND/OR H:YOURS DO NO
       T GIVE"
1100   PRINT "A SUCCESSFUL CENTRE
       TO"
1110   PRINT "CENTRE TRAJECTORY."
1120   PRINT
1140   GOTO 420
9999   END
```

Results

```
THIS PROGRAM TESTS WHETHER
A BASKETBALL FREE THROW WILL
BE SUCCESSFUL.
YOU NEED ONLY INPUT A VALUE
OF RELEASE VELOCITY V(MS-1)
AND REL.HEIGHT H(M).

THE PROGRAM COMPUTES THE TWO
RESULTING RELEASE ANGLES A1
AND A2 (DEG) FOR WHICH THE
CENTRE OF THE BALL WILL PASS
THROUGH THE CENTRE OF THE HOOP

THESE TWO RELEASE ANGLES ARE
THEN USED TO CALC. B1 AND B2
(DEG),THE CONSEQUENT ANGLES OF
ATTEMPTED ENTRY TO THE HOOP.

THE GEOMETRY OF BALL ENTRY TO
HOOP SHOWS THAT ENTRY IS
IMPOSSIBLE UNLESS
    ANGLE OF ENTRY>33.14 DEG.

WHATEVER THE OUTCOME OF YOUR
FREE THROW,A SUITABLE MESSAGE
IS PRINTED!
```

```
FOR REL.VEL.V(MS-1)=8
AND REL.HT. H(M)=2.25

THE TWO POSS.REL.ANG. ARE

A1(DEG)=64.9339654A2(DEG)=34.9319259

THE TWO ASSOC.ANGLES OF
ENTRY ARE

B1(DEG)=77.330077B2(DEG)=22.8321275

GREAT SHOT-YOU SCORED!
```

```
WHAT IS REL.VEL. (MS-1) OF
BASKETBALL?
SENSIBLE RANGE: 6-9 MS-1.
ENTER VALUE,PRESS RETURN.
?8
WHAT IS REL.HT. (M) OF
BASKETBALL?
SENSIBLE RANGE:2.0-2.75 M.
ENTER VALUE,PRESS RETURN.
?1.9


FOR REL.VEL.V(MS-1)=8
AND REL.HT. H(M)=1.9

THE TWO POSS.REL.ANG. ARE

A1(DEG)=63.0644884A2(DEG)=40.971843

THE TWO ASSOC.ANGLES OF
ENTRY ARE

B1(DEG)=26.9191248B2(DEG)=30.3474794

BAD LUCK-YOU MISSED-NO POINTS!



    .


WHAT IS REL.VEL. (MS-1) OF
BASKETBALL?
SENSIBLE RANGE: 6-9 MS-1.
ENTER VALUE,PRESS RETURN.
?6
WHAT IS REL.HT. (M) OF
BASKETBALL?
SENSIBLE RANGE:2.0-2.75 M.
ENTER VALUE,PRESS RETURN.
?1.75


TRY DIFFERENT VALUES OF V
AND/OR H:YOURS DO NOT GIVE
A SUCCESSFUL CENTRE TO
CENTRE TRAJECTORY.
```

```
FOR REL.VEL.V(MS-1)=7.75
AND REL.HT. H(M)=2.2

THE TWO POSS.REL.ANG. ARE

A1(DEG)=61.7337816A2(DEG)=38.7354776

THE TWO ASSOC.ANGLES OF
ENTRY ARE

B1(DEG)=79.8390295B2(DEG)=50.3446549

GREAT SHOT-YOU SCORED!
```

Index

Acceleration,
  angular, of ball, 146, 147
  of runner, 13, 14, 16, 25
  versus velocity, 26, 27
Aerodynamic drag force,
  on boat, 88
  on discus, 46
  on javelin, 46
  on long jumper, 71
  on skier, 94, 95, 97
Aerodynamic force on sail, 110, 113, 114,
  116, 117, 126, 128
Aerodynamic shapes, 46
Aerofoil, 110, 116, 123
Airflow,
  laminar, 113
  over sail, 128
  turbulent, 108
  viscous effects of, 110
Air resistance effects,
  on discus, 46
  on hurdler, 30
  on javelin, 46
  on long jumper, 68, 71
  on motion of a ball, 147–157
  on runner, 16, 18, 23, 30
  on shot, 36, 37
Americas Cup, 121
Amplitude of arm action in running, 23
Angle of entry of basketball to hoop, 47,
  49, 187
Angle of heel of yacht, 113
Angle of incidence,
  oblique impact, 140
  of sail, 114, 117, 118, 131, 132, 133
  of wing, 108
  stalled, 118
Angle of reflection, oblique impact, 141
Angle of release of basketball, 50, 187

Angular velocity, 18, 22, 69, 74
  of ball, 147
  of bat, 155
  of gymnast, 107
  of hammer, 42
  of ice skater, 104, 105
  of triple jumper's leg, 75

Ball,
  spinning, 120
  temperature of, 140
Banana shot, 153
Baseball, 136, 142, 150, 163
BASIC computer programs,
  free throw in basketball, 50, 187–195
  hammer throw, 46, 171–179
  long jump, 67, 171–179
  moment of inertia of runner's leg, 21,
    165–170
  optimum angle of release, 46, 180–186
  shot put, 36, 171–179
Basketball, 47–51
  ball diameter, 47
  free throw regulations, 47, 48
  maximum height reached, 50
  see also Throwing
Batsman, 163
Batter, 163, 164
Beam, of boat, 92, 121
Bends, banked, 16
Bernoulli, 108
Blunt shaped body, 23
Bottomspin, 148, 152
Bounce pass, in basketball, 140
Boundary layer, 119, 120
Bounding action, in triple jump, 74
Bowler, cricket, 154, 159, 163
Braking effect, 30, 74

Brancazio, P. J., 163
Bullet start technique, 14, 15
Buoyancy force,
 on windsurfer, 126
 on yacht, 115

Centre of mass,
 of bat, 155
 of clubhead, 149
 of high jumper, 52, 53, 54, 56, 57, 58
 of hurdler, 30
 of long jumper, 66, 68
 of pole vaulter, 60, 61, 63, 66
 of runner, 16, 18
 of snooker ball, 145, 150
 of windsurfer, 123
Centrifugal force, in hammer throw, 40
Centripetal force, in hammer throw, 16, 39
Chord length, of sail, 110, 117, 132
Circular cylinder, use in model of athlete,
 18, 21, 101, 102, 103, 165, 166
Clearance, of hurdle, 30
Cornering, 31
Correlation coefficient, 26, 79
Countering, in hammer throw,
 with hips, 40
 with upper body, 40
Courageous, 120
Crews,
 coxed, 93
 coxless, 93
Cricket, 136, 142, 154, 163
 batsman, 163
 bowler, 154, 159, 163
Cross product, see Vector product

Darts, 98–101,
 double, 99
 single, 99
 throw, definition of, 99
 treble, 99
Density, air, 108
 variation with altitude, 71
Differential, use as an approximation, 38, 97
Differential equations, first order
 initial condition, 24
 integrating factor, 95, 96
 numerical solution of, 37
 simultaneous, 37
 variables separable, 23, 25, 72, 96
Differentiation, 38, 45, 49, 50, 54, 97
Dip, of path of cricket ball, 157
Discus, 46
Displacement, of yacht, 120
Distance-time data, 14, 25

Distance travelled, 23
Diving, 101–107
Downhill skiing, 23, 94–97
Drag coefficient, 71, 95
Drag force
 on ball, 155
 on boat, 92, 117
 on sail, 116, 117
 on shot, 36
 on skier, 94, 95
 reduction of, 120, 163
Draught, of yacht, 121
Drift, 116
Drive phase, of running action, 16, 17, 18,
 30
Driving force
 constant for a sprinter, 24
 of hurdler, 30
 of runner, 16
 on sail, 110, 113, 114, 116, 117, 132, 133
 on sailing vessel, origin of, 108, 110

Egg position, of skier, 97
Eights, rowing
 German rig, 91, 92
 Italian rig, 91, 92
 traditional rig, 91
Elasticity, 137
Ellipse, 47
Elongated start technique, 14, 15
End plates, 123
Energy
 conservation of, applied to ball, 138, 139
 applied to pole vault, 59, 60
 expenditure in static work, 76
 kinetic, applied to pole vault, 59, 66
 of rotation, 106
 loss of, due to waves, 120
 of runner, 24
 potential, stored in pole vault pole, 58,
 61, 64
 stored in spring, 58
Equation of motion, see Newton's second
 law of motion
Equilibrium, 31, 123

Fatigue effects
 in steeple chase, 33
 on stride length, 31
Fins, see wing keel
Fitness, measurement of, 81
Football, American, 136
Forces acting in
 ballgames, 142, 145, 146, 155, 156, 157
 discus throw, 46
 hammer throw, 39, 40

Forces acting in – continued
  hurdling, 30, 31
  javelin throw, 46
  long jumping, 68, 69, 71
  pole vault, 61, 63, 64, 65
  rowing, 88–90
  running, 16, 17, 23, 24
  shot put, 34, 36, 37
  skiing, 94
  yachting, 110, 113–117, 119, 132, 133
  windsurfing, 123–128
Forward inclination of body, 17
Forward pass, Rugby football, 157–159
Fours, rowing
  Italian rig, 90
  traditional rig, 89
Free shot, in basketball, 47, 50, 188
Free throw line, in basketball, 48, 50, 187
Friction
  between ball and table, 145
  coefficient of sliding, 94, 146
Froude, law of comparison, 120

Golf
  dimpled surface of ball, 136
  hooked shot, 152
  sliced shot, 136, 148, 152
Gravity, 30, 35, 60, 66, 71, 72, 94, 171, 180
Gymnastics, 53, 101–107
  somersault, 106, 107
  tucking, 107

Hammer throwing, 38–44
  countering, 40
  description of event, 38
  dimensions, 38
  leading, 40
  measurement of throw, 44
  three dimensional model, 39, 42, 44
  two dimensional model, 39, 40
  world record, 171
Handstand, 66
Hang, 69, 70, 75
Harvard Index, definition of, 82
Harvard step test
  basic description, 81
  Modifications for different groups by age
    and sex, 82, 83
Heel, 116
  angle of, 113
Heeling force, 114, 116, 117, 123
Heeling moment, 114

High jump, 52–58
  biomechanical model of jumper, 55
  techniques
    Fosbury flop, 52, 53, 57
    scissors, 52
    straddle, 52
Hips, 18, 40
Hitch kick, 69, 70, 74, 75
Hooked shot, 152
Hop, step and jump, see Triple jump
Horizontal circle, motion in a, 38
Hull, V-shaped, 121
Human body
  changes in position while jumping, 55, 56, 60, 61, 63, 64, 68, 69, 70
  changes in position while running, 16
  five segment model of, 102
  ten segment model of, 55
  surface area of, 83
Hurdle
  approved, 31
  heights of, 29
  spacing, 29, 30
Hurdling, 28–31
  events, 28, 29
  safety in, 31
  stages in
    clearance, 30
    landing, 30
    take-off, 29
Hydrodynamic drag force on a boat, 92

Ice skating, 101–107
Impact
  direct, 140
  oblique, 140, 142, 143
Impulse of high jumper at take-off, 53, 57, 58
Impulsive blow, 145
Impulsive reaction, 154, 155
Inclination of runner's body, 16
Integration, 40, 54, 72, 147
  by parts, 131
  by substitution, 96
  double, 114, 128, 130, 131
  see also differential equations and
    Simpson's rule
International Olympic Committee, 91
Isometric exercise, 76
Isotonic contraction, 76
Isotonic exercise, 76

Javelin, 46
Jib, 113
Jumping, 52–75

Keel, 114, 116, 123
  winged, 121–123
Kinetic energy, *see* Energy

Laminar flow, 113, 157
Lanchester, F. W., 116, 123
Landing
  in hurdling, 30
  in long jump, 66, 68, 69
Leading leg, in hurdling, 30
Leading with hands, in hammer throwing,
    40, 42
Leaning into bend by runner, 16
Leeway, 110
Leg action of runner, phases in
  drive, 17, 18
  recovery, 17, 18
  support, 17
Leg action in long jumping, 66
Lift force
  on ball, 150
  on discus, 46
  on javelin, 46
  on long jumper, 68
  on planing yacht, 121
  on windsurfing sail, 128
  on wing, 108
Lift, vertical on high jumper, 53
Lift, vertical on long jumper, 68
Lillee, D., 164
Line of action of force, 123
Line of best fit, 26, 79
Linear regression, method of, 26, 79
Lofted clubs, 150
Logarithms, 78, 93
Long distance events, 13, 18, 23, 26, 30
Long jump, 66–73
  measurement of length of, 66
  phases in
    approach, 68
    landing, 68, 69
    take-off, 68
  styles
    hang, 69, 70, 75
    hitch kick, 69, 70, 74, 75
    sail, 69
  world record, 68, 70, 171

Maclaurin expansion of logarithm function,
    73
Magnus force, 150, 151, 152, 153, 154, 163
Main sail, 113
Marathoner, 13, 28
Mathematical model
  of gymnast, 101

Mathematical model – continued
  of ice skater, 101
  of runner's leg, 18, 21, 165
  of running, 23
Maximum value, determination of, 45
Mean value, 87
Medium start technique, 14, 15
Metronome, 63
Middle distance events, 13, 18, 23, 26, 30
Middle distance runner, 165
Moment of force
  applied to heeling, 114
  applied to hurdling, 31
  applied to pole vault, 61, 65
  applied to rowing, 89, 90
  applied to runner, 16, 17
  applied to windsurfing, 123, 126
Moment of inertia
  definition, 101
  of composite body, 105
  of circular cylinder, 21, 102, 165, 166
  of gymnast, 106, 107
  of hurdler's leg, 29
  of ice skater, 104, 105, 106
  of long jumper's body, 69
  of long jumper's leg, 69, 75
  of runner's leg, 18, 21, 22, 165
  of sphere, 146, 155
Momentum, angular
  conservation of
    in gymnastics, 106
    in hammer throw, 40
    in iceskating, 105, 106
    in long jump, 66, 69, 70
    in pole vault, 63
    in running, 18
  definition, of 18
  of diver, 101
  of gymnast, 101, 106, 107
  of hammer thrower, 40
  of iceskater, 105
  of leg, 18, 22, 29
Momentum, linear
  conservation of
    in high jump, 53
    in impacts in ball games, 142
    in long jump, 66, 69
  of gymnast, 106
  of hull, 120
  of long jumper, 66, 69
  of steeplechaser, 33
  of triple jumper, 73
Muscles, 24, 28, 76

New Scientist, 163
Newton's law of impact, 137, 142

Newton's second law of motion
    applied to hammer throw, 40
        high jump, 53
        long jump, 71
        motion of ball, 146
        runner, 23
        shot put, 36
        skiing, 95
Newton's third law of motion
    applied to hammer throw, 40
        long jump, 69
Nomogram, 83
Numerical integration, 14, 37

Oar arrangements, 88–92
Oarsmen
    number in a boat, 92, 93
    optimum positioning of, 88–92
Optimisation
    applied to rowing, 88–92
    applied to running, 24
Optimum angle of release, 44, 46, 180
Overreach of stride in hurdling, 31
Oxygen
    in the blood, 24, 28
    rate of supply of, 24

Parallel axes theorem, 21, 102, 104, 105, 155, 166
Percussion, centre of, 154
Pitcher, baseball, 150, 163
Pole vault, 58–66
    carry of pole, 65, 66
    construction of pole, 59
    description of event, 58, 59
    free end of pole, 59
    length of pole, 64
    stages in
        clearance, 64
        plant, 61
        pull up, 64
        run up, 60
        swing and rock back, 63
        take-off, 61
        world record, 60
Position vector, 42
Potential energy, see Energy
Power, definition of, 92
Prandtl, 119
Pressure
    air, 108, 110, 118
    centre of, 114, 126, 128–131
    difference, 110
    distribution over sail, 110
    relative intensity, 110

Probability
    defined as relative frequency, 99
    laws of, 99, 100
Projectile model
    of basketball free throw, 48, 49, 50
    of hammer throw, 44
    of high jump, 53
    of long jump, 67, 71
    of runner, 18
    of shotput, 34, 35, 36
    time of flight, 160
    wind effects on range of, 160, 161
Propulsive force
    of runner, 23
    maximum, 24
Pulse ratio tests, 81
Pumping, 131–133

Radius of bend, 16
Range
    of hammer throw, 38, 40, 44, 45, 171
    of long jump projectile phase, 66, 67, 72, 73, 171
    of shot put, 34, 35, 44, 45, 171
    maximum value, using differentiation, 45
Reaction force, 17, 18
Recovery phase of runner's stride, 17, 18, 22
Relative velocity, 133–135
    direction of 134
    of ball with respect to wind, 159, 162
    magnitude of, 134
    in Rugby football, 157, 158
Release angle, optimum value of
    in hammer, 44
    in shot, 44
Release parameters, values of
    basketball, 49, 50, 188
    hammer, 38, 39, 42, 171, 180
    long jump, 67, 171, 180
    shot, 34, 35, 171, 180
Release velocity
    of baseball, 163
    of cricket ball, 163
Resistance to motion
    of boat, 88
    of runner, 18, 23
    of shot, 36
    of skier, 95
Restitution, coefficient of, 137, 139
    effect of temperature on, 140
Reynolds number, 119
Rolling of balls, 145, 146, 154
    condition for, 147
Rotation
    backwards of runner, 16
    effects of air resistance force on, 16

Rotation – continued
fixed axis of
gymnastics, 101
iceskating, 101
running, 21, 22
forwards of
hurdler, 29
long jumper, 69, 70
pole vaulter, 61, 64
runner, 16
triple jumper, 75
kinetic energy of, *see* Energy
moving axis of
diving, 101
gymnastics, 101
of runner on bend, 16
of runner's leg, 165
of runner's hips, 22
of runner's shoulders, 22, 23
speed of, 29
Rugby, 136

Sailing, 108–135
Scale factor, 119
Separation
delay of, 120, 157, 163
of airflow around ball, 155
point of, 110, 113, 120
Shot put, 34–38
mass of shot, 37
world record, 36, 171
Simpson's rule, 14
Skidding of ball, 144–147
duration of, 146
Skin friction
coefficient of, 120
resistance, 120
Sliced shot
golf, 136, 148, 152
tennis, 148
Slope
of distance-time curve, 14, 25
of velocity-time curve, 25
of tangent, 14, 25
of trajectory, 49
Snooker, 136, 142
Soccer, 136, 153
Somersault, 106, 107
Spin
acquiring of, 148, 149
axis of, 148
of ball, 144–147
rate of, 163
Sprinter, 13, 165
Sprints, 13, 23, 24, 29, 30, 68
Squash, 136

Stability
of javelin, 46
of pole vaulter during run up, 60
of runner, 22
of triple jumper at take-off, 74
of yacht, 113
Standard deviation, 87
Starting blocks, 13, 16, 29
Starting techniques, 13, 14, 15, 16
bullet, 14, 15
elongated, 14, 15
medium, 14, 15, 16
Steeplechase, 31–33
rules of, 31
barriers, 31
take-off velocity, 33
water jump, 31, 33
Streamline, 108, 150
Streamlined shape, 23, 95, 118
Stride frequency, 13, 16, 30, 31
Stride length, 13, 16, 18
Stride pattern, 29
Support phase, leg action in running, 17
Surface area
of human body, 83
of wetted hull, 92
presented by long jumper, 71
presented by skier, 94

t-test, 87
Table tennis, 148, 151
Tactics, in running, 23, 26
Take-off phase in
high jump, 53, 55, 57
hurdles, 29
long jump, 66, 68, 69
pole vault, 61
triple jump, 74
Take-off velocity of
high jumper, 53
hurdler, 30
long jumper, 67
runner, 18
steeple chaser, 33
triple jumper, 74
Tangent, slope of, 14, 25
Tennis, 148, 151
Terminal velocity, of skier, 95, 96, 97
Throwing, 34–51
of basketball, 47–51
of discus, 46
of hammer, 38–44
of javelin, 46
of shot, 34–38, 51
Throwing area, shot put event, 37

Thrust
  of high jumper at take-off, 53, 58
  of runner's leg, 18
  on sail, 130
Toe-to-toe distance, 13, 14
Topspin, 148, 151, 152
Track events
  non sprint, 28
  sprint, 25
Trailing edge, 118
Trailing leg, in hurdling, 30
Trajectory
  of ball, 148
  of basketball, 49, 50, 187
  of centre of mass of long jumper, 66, 69
  of centre of mass of runner, 18
  of shot, 34, 37
  parabolic, 136
Trim, of yacht, 114
Triple jump, 73–75
  rules, 73
  stages in
    approach run, 74
    hop, 74
    jump, 75
    step, 75
    take-off, 74
  styles
    Polish, 74
    Russian, 74
Tucking, 107
Turbulence, 108, 110, 136, 163
  induced, 120
Turbulent flow, 157
Twist, of sail, 118

Under reach of stride in hurdling, 31

Vector product, 42
Velocity, 25, 26, 28, 29
  first and second power of, 23
  see also angular velocity

Velocity-time curve, 25
Viscosity, coefficient of kinematic, 119
Viscous forces on a boat, 88, 91
Vortex, 121, 123

Wake, 110
  eddying, 118
  of airflow around ball, 155, 156
  turbulent, 120
Water jump, in steeple chase, 33
Waterline length, 120
Wave
  bow, 121
  resistance, 120
Wind
  relative velocity of, 133
  true velocity of, 133
Wind effects
  on ball games, 159–162
  on discus, 46
  on javelin, 46
  on rowing, 91
Wind speed, variation with height, 117, 162
Windsurfer, 123, 125
Windsurfing, 114, 123–128
Wind tunnel tests
  on balls, 155
  on skiers, 97
Windward, sailing to, 113, 116
Wing, aircraft, 108, 110
  slotted, 113
  span, 121
  tips, 121
Winged keel, 121–123
Work done, definition of, 76
World records
  hammer, 171
  long jump, 68, 70, 171
  pole vault, 60
  shot, 36, 171

Yacht, 110, 113, 114, 116, 120, 121, 123
  planing, 121